natural
DESIGNS

Contemporary Organic Upcycling

natural
DESIGNS

Contemporary Organic Upcycling

AURÉLIE DROUET
photography JÉRÔME BLIN
illustrations JEAN-MARIE REYMOND

SCRIPTUM
EDITIONS

CONTENTS

DESIGNS

DESIGNER PROFILES

APPENDICES

NTRODUCTION

'Human ingenuity may use a variety of tools to produce numerous inventions contributing to the same ends, but it will never devise anything more beautiful, simpler or more perfectly adapted to its purpose than does nature; for in the inventions of nature, nothing is lacking and nothing is superfluous.'

Leonardo da Vinci

Since the dawn of time, nature has been a source of inexhaustible inspiration. Painters, designers, poets, musicians and architects alike have all found a vehicle of expression for their art in nature. Nature is everywhere, all around us and within us. Its shapes and materials inspire the creative spirit in all of us. From the largest objects to the smallest—from an aircraft wing inspired by a bird's wing to furniture based on the structure of a flower or shaped by a tree trunk—nature has always inspired artists and designers, and always will.

This is the philosophy that is the inspiration for Natural Design: making use of natural materials to create furniture and other everyday objects. The designers of these projects have harnessed the qualities of wood, slate, wool, bamboo, hemp, cotton, cork, and more to create designs to enable us to furnish our living spaces with authentic materials, whether mineral or plant-based.

They encourage us to let our imaginations roam free, through woodland glades or along the sea shore, bringing nature into our living rooms with twenty designs – practical, decorative and durable – presented here in easy-to-follow instructions. From a cork pendant light to a slate-topped table, from a crochet wool pouffe to a coat rack made out of silver birch, these simple creations display all the beauty and subtle colours of authentic natural materials in their untreated state. Environmentally friendly and in harmony with nature, these are designs that are not only unusual and inventive, but that also boast the distinction of being 100% natural.

TIPS AND POINTERS

To build the designs

For each design you will find a list of the tools and materials required to make it. As the basic toolkit is not repeated each time, here is a list of the tools that you will need to keep to hand:

tape measure
good quality carpenter's pencil
metal rule and set square
gloves, safety glasses/goggles and mask
flat screwdriver and a Phillips screwdriver
hammers (various sizes)
pliers (various)
paintbrushes and rollers: round, sash, flat, mini-roller

Measurements for nails, screws and nuts are for guidance only, to be adapted according to the thickness of the boards and the material of the wall (wood, stone, plasterboard etc.).

Electrical installations

Special care must always be taken with any electrical installation. Always check the specifications of electrical products carefully before purchasing them, and if in doubt seek professional advice.

To create your own designs

All the designs suggested here are basic models from which you can improvise your own designs. Let you imagination run wild!

Readers are invited to send photographs of their own designs inspired by this book to the author at:
aureliedrouet@free.fr

NATURAL MATERIALS

The principal natural materials used in this book:

Hemp (1)

Hemp is the strongest of all natural plant fibres. Used from earliest times to make fabrics and rope, and later paper, hemp has antibacterial and antifungal properties and is soft and breathable. It also holds its shape, and is resistant to shrinkage, light and heat. Its possible applications in interior design are manifold.

Wood (2)

Wood is the structural tissue found in the branches, trunk and roots of trees. Of the sixty thousand woody plant species that grow worldwide, some six thousand are used for wood for building construction and furniture-making. Each species has its specific properties, which determine its main uses: oak is extremely dense, for instance, and pine is very hard, while poplar is light. Synonymous as it is with warmth and authenticity, wood is the material chosen par excellence to give a 'natural' look to interiors.

Slate (3)

Most familiar as a roof covering, slate has now into our interiors, where it is used for floors, work surfaces and decorative objects. Slate is a shale-like, natural rock that occurs in a rich variety of colours, from blue to black and from red to green, that never fade or change. Easy to work and maintain, strong and fine-grained, slate has numerous qualities to recommend it.

Bamboo (4)

Botanically neither a tree nor a shrub, bamboo is in fact the largest member of the grass family, prized by architects and designers for its lightness, flexibility and remarkably high compressive and tensile strength. Used not just for construction but also for culinary and everyday utensils, musical instruments, floors, furniture, clothing and as a food source, this versatile and extremely fast-growing plant is cultivated widely throughout Asia.

Wool (5)

Wool is an animal fibre obtained from the fleece of sheep, goats (cashmere and mohair), rabbits (angora) and certain other animals such as camels. Pure virgin wool can only be obtained by clipping from healthy living animals. Other types of wool may be recycled. Wool is a strong, warm and highly elastic fibre that is used both as a wadding for mattresses and in furnishing fabrics.

Cork (6)

Cork is harvested from the bark of certain trees, particularly the cork oak. Its thickness, impermeability and lightness make it the most effective material for insulation. But in addition to being useful for walls and floors, it also offers aesthetic and technical qualities that are valued by artists and designers. Renewable, durable and recyclable, cork is a material for the future.

2.

4.

6.

1.

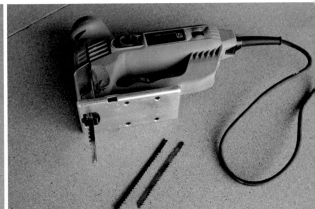

2.

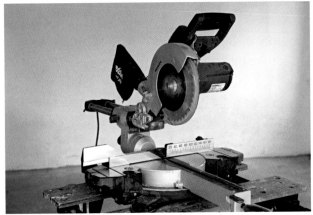

3.

4.

5.

6.

TOOL GUIDE

Basic protective equipment (1)

The use of gloves, a mask (even for sanding) and sometimes safety glasses is seriously recommended. This basic equipment is indispensable for protecting the hands and face when using certain tools and handling chemical products. We also advise using products that respect the environment, and that will consequently also respect the user's health.

Jigsaw (2)

To ensure that you get the best use out of your jigsaw, make sure you choose one that can cut different thicknesses of wood, and has variable speeds and an adjustable base plate (up to 45 degrees) for making cuts on sloping surfaces. Choose the right blade for the material you want to saw. Observe the necessary safety precautions, and the jigsaw will help you to work accurately and safely.

Radial arm saw (3)

The radial arm saw is ideal for precision cutting of numerous materials, including wood, plastic, slate and steel. We would recommend a sliding mitre saw, a 'mobile' version that is easier to use, less costly and more practical as it can be transported. A multitude of blades is available for different functions.

Orbital sander (4)

The orbital sander has a random-orbit circular disc that is useful for both rough and fine sanding. Light and easy to use, it can be used on all surfaces except angles. Wear a dust mask, gloves and safety glasses. Always sand in the direction of the grain. A well-sanded surface should be smooth to the touch.

Eccentric sander (5)

The eccentric sander has a rotating circular sanding surface designed for both coarse and fine sanding for a perfect finish. Light and easy to handle, it can be used on all surfaces except corners. Wear a dust mask, gloves and safety glasses, and always sand along the grain. When a surface is properly sanded it should be smooth to the touch.

Detail sander (6)

The detail or corner sander is an orbital sander that is ideal for finishing. The shape and small dimensions of its sanding surface make it highly practical for sanding small areas that are flat but 'distressed', and for reaching awkward spots, and it is both light and very easy to use.

TOOL GUIDE (CONT.)

Wire strippers (7)

Electrical work invariably involves stripping wires. Use wire strippers to make this job easier. A locking screw allows you to adjust the blades according to the gauge of the wire, so that you can strip the insulating cover without any risk of damaging the wire.

Holesaw (8)

The holesaw is indispensable for sawing circular openings. Choose the size appropriate to the size of your openings and a blade designed for the materal to be cut (wood, plasterboard, concrete, etc.). The holesaw is attached to a drill, like a bit. Place the guide bit over the centre of the hole to be cut and drill slowly, taking care to hold the drill perpendicular to obtain an even cut. Sand the edges of the hole to finish.

Glue gun (9)

The glue gun is an accurate way to glue all types of material, including wood, card, textiles and aluminium. The mains power versions are the most effective at melting the hot glue sticks. The glue gun is easy to use and has many uses, dispensing the glue in a line of a diameter set by the nozzle. As the drying time is very quick, the parts need to be assembled while the glue is still hot. Take care not to touch the hot glue, and wait until the gun has cooled before cleaning the nozzle.

Power multi-tool (10)

Whether for drilling, countersinking, grinding, cuttin or even engraving, the power multi-tools are invaluabl for delicate or detailed work. Compact, ergonomic an popular with model-makers, they are easy to handle an very accurate to use. The numerous accessories tha are available (for routing, polishing, sanding, cutting etc make this the ideal tool for creative hobbies.

Paintbrushes and rollers (11)

Brushes are available in different sizes and materia for different uses. For fiddly jobs such as cutting i we recommend using a sash brush, which is pointe Flat brushes are used for varnishing and lacquerin For varnishing or painting large flat surfaces, use mini-roller. The end result you obtain will depend o your choice of paintbrush or roller, so always ask fo professional advice when buying.

Countersink bit (12)

The countersink bit is used to countersink holes (conic tip) or straight lines and curves (cylindrical tip). I woodwork, it is useful for removing any burrs aroun the holes to ensure that screw heads are concealed (it principal use in this book).

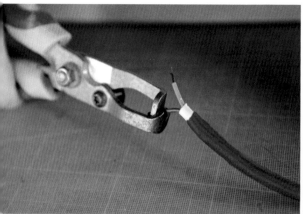

8.

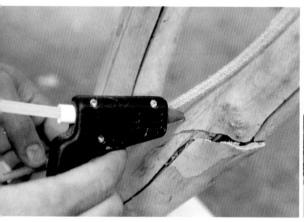

10.

12.

AMBROISE

Console tables are redolent of a grander and more sumptuous age, but now – thanks to contemporary designers – they are enjoying a new lease of life.

Their slim profile makes them ideal for fitting snugly into halls and passageways.

From its base inspired by branching tree boughs to the subtle relief of its slate top, *Ambroise* offers a natural take on classical elegance.

DESIGN BY:
JEAN-MARIE REYMOND

AMBROISE

TOOLBOX	
Tools	**Materials**
<ul><li>Radial arm saw</li><li>Cordless drill</li><li>Clamps</li><li>Steel square</li><li>Spatula knife</li><li>Small sash brush</li></ul>	<ul><li>1 sheet MDF (120 (3'11") x 35 (1' 1³/₄") x 1.5cm (⁵/₈"))</li><li>5 pine battens without knots (250 (8' 2¹/₂") x 3 (1¹/₈") x 3cm (1¹/₈"))</li><li>10 slates (40 (1' 3³/₄") x 22cm (8³/₄"))</li><li>Wood screws</li><li>Wood filler</li><li>Wood glue</li><li>Black silicone glue</li><li>Black and white paint</li></ul>

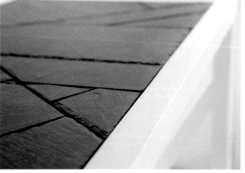

Telling details: The base recalls the branches of a tree, while the slates provide a gentle relief.

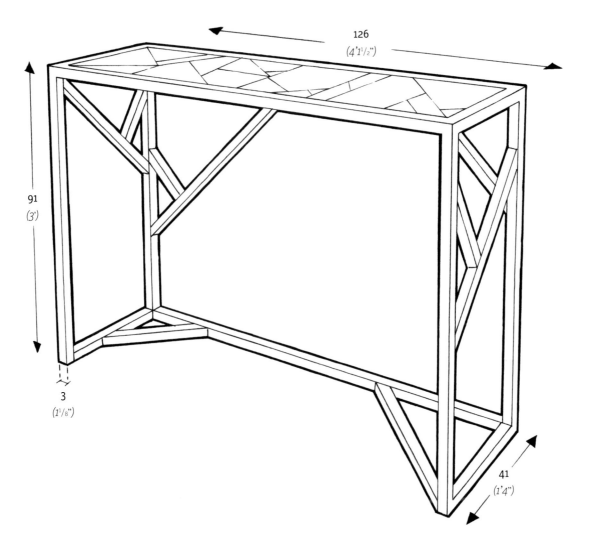

126
(4'1¹/₂")

91
(3')

3
(1¹/₈")

41
(1'4")

All measurements are in centimetres and inches (to nearest fraction).

Step-by-step-guide

CONSOLE TOP

1. For the frame, saw 2 x 126cm *(4'1½")* lengths of batten (= length of top + [2 x depth of the wood]) and 2 x 41cm *(1'4")* lengths (= width of top + [2 x depth of the wood]).
Cut the ends at 45 degrees

2. To ensure the upper surface of the slates is flush with the wood, draw a line around the inside of the frame equal to the depth of the slates (usually around 5mm *(³/₁₆")*) and the glue (around 2mm *(⁵/₆₄")*).

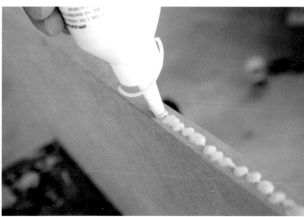

3. Pre-drill pilot holes in the battens, then countersink the holes to conceal the screw heads.

4. Glue the edges of the MDF.

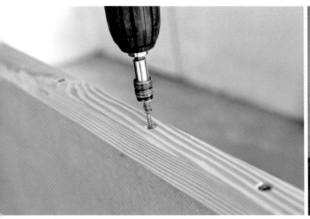

5. Screw the wood to the MDF. Take care to position the top of the MDF along the line drawn in step 2.
Paint the MDF with 2 coats of black paint.

<u>CONSOLE BASE</u>

6. Cut the remainder of the battens as follows:
— 4 x 88cm *(2'11")* and 2 x 35cm *(1' 1³/₄")* to make the U shapes;
— 1 x 120cm *(3'11")* for the rear strut.
Screw and glue together the Us and the rear strut, using wood filler where necessary.

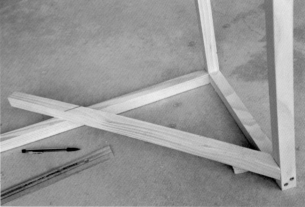

7. Assemble the top and base, taking care to pre-drill pilot holes every piece and countersink the holes before inserting the screws.

8. To ensure stability, add corner struts between the U-shapes sand the rear struts. Take a length of batten and cut one end at 45 degrees. Place this against the front of the base and mark the angle at which it meets the rear strut. Cut along this line, pre-drill and countersink pilot holes and screw in position.

Step-by-step-guide

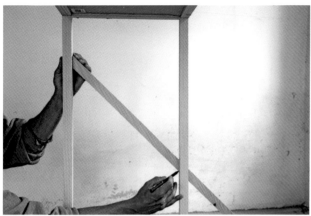

9. Add the long diagonal battens as in Step 8.

10. Add the shorter battens by placing them in the desired position and marking the cuts for the ends.

11. Pre-drill and countersink pilot holes in the battens and screw together, using wood filler as necessary.

SLATE TOP

12. Position the first slate in one of the corners of the top, then use a nail to mark 2 lines to give the desired shape.

13. Use a radial arm saw with care to cut the slate.

14. Put the cut slate back in place, then position another piece of slate to make the next cut. Continue to complete the slate top.

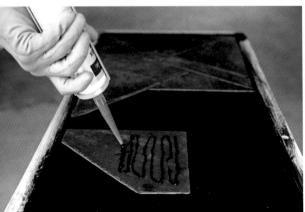

15. Use black silicone glue to glue the slates in place. Allow to dry before moving the table.

PAINTING

16. Create a black-and-white contrast by painting the base with a light undercoat and white top coat, using a small sash brush.

VASCO

DESIGN

Shaped by wind and tide, washed up on the shoreline after a long sea voyage,
driftwood is a natural raw material that has a romantic tale to tell.

The softness of naturally distressed wood and the natural design of the branch lend *Vasco* its special quality,
which needs virtually no addition to be transformed into a standard lamp.
Just a lampshade and some cable will suffice to transform it into a contemporary and timeless lamp,
to complement every style of interior decor.

DESIGN BY:
JEAN-MARIE REYMOND

TECHNICAL CONSULTANTS:
FALBALA LUMINAIRES

VASCO

TOOLBOX

Tools

- Jigsaw
- Holesaw
- Cordless drill
- Wire cutters
- Glue gun
- Trowel
- Wood rasp + fine sandpaper
- Electrical screwdriver
- Spirit level
- Vaseline
- Retractable knife

Materials

- 1 forked branch of driftwood
- 3 lampshades
- Transparent Perspex insulating covers
- 5m (16') cable + electrical components (cable clips, lamp holders, connector strip)
- 1 30 x 30cm (1') sheet of MDF
- 1 60 x 60cm (2') timber base
- 1 10kg (22lb) sack ready-mixed sand and cement
- 1 5kg (11lb) sack gravel
- 35cm (1' 1³/₄")-diameter plastic bucket

Telling details: Gently distressed wood makes a perfect natural floor lamp.

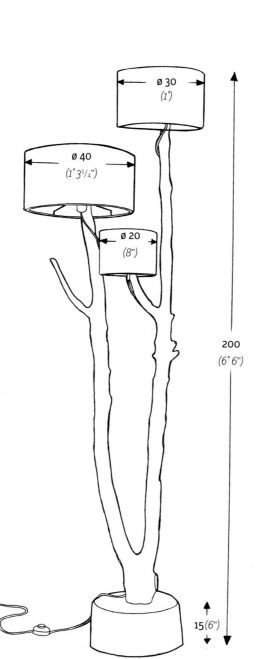

ø 30
(1')

ø 40
(1' 3³/₄")

ø 20
(8")

200
(6' 6")

15 (6")

All measurements are in centimetres and inches (to nearest fraction).

Step-by-step-guide

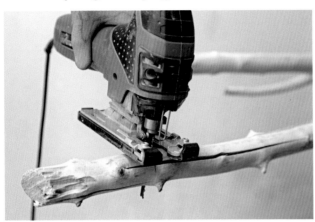

1. Cut the branches of the driftwood to the desired length and level the base.

2. Prop the branch against a board or table, taking care to keep the base level. Tie it in place, making sure it is vertical so that the lampshades will be horizontal when attached.

3. Make the 3 MDF brackets for the lampshades. Draw a circle on each to fit the lamp holders.

4. Cut out the circles with a holesaw.

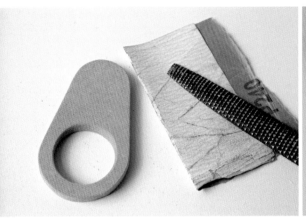

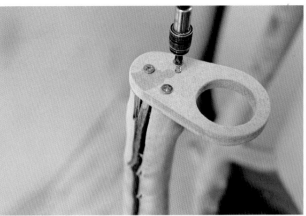

5. Cut around the brackets with a jigsaw and sand the edges with fine sandpaper. If necessary, use a wood rasp to adjust the size of the holes.

6. Pre-drill and countersink the brackets and screw them to the driftwood. Use a spirit level to check they are horizontal.

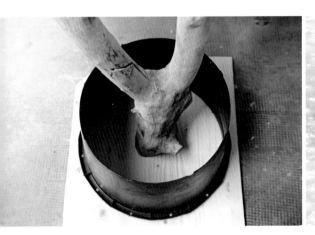

7. Make the mould for the lamp base. Cut the top off the bucket to a depth of 20cm(8") and discard the bottom. Clean the top well and screw it to the 60 x 60cm(2') timber base. Smear the inside with Vaseline, then position the driftwood in the centre.

8. Make the cement and add gravel.

Step-by-step-guide

9. Pour the cement mixture into the mould, tapping the sides as you go to bring any air bubbles to the surface.

10. Remove the bucket from the timber base, cutting it carefully with a Retractable knife. Sand the cement with fine sandpaper.

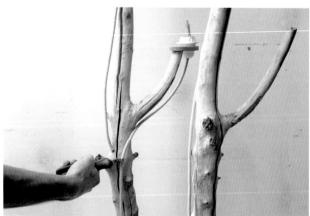

11. Cut the cable to length.

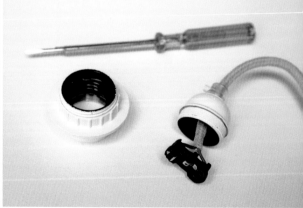

12. Wire the lamp holders following stages 7 to 11 of Sunrise, pp. 71–72, then insert them in the brackets

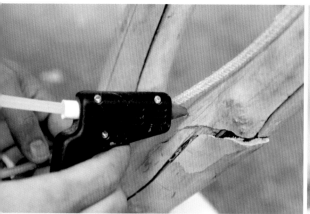

13. Run lines of glue down the driftwood with a glue gun, then glue the cable to the driftwood.

14. Connect up the cable using the connector strip.

15. Screw transparent Perspex insulating covers to the driftwood to protect the connector strip.

16. Wire the foot switch and plug according to the manufacturer's instructions.

Jean-Marie Reymond
Designer

Jean-Marie in 5 dates

1981: Born in Saint-Nazaire.

1997: Spends a year in America.

2006: Graduates in interior design and architecture at the Ecole Pivaut, Nantes.

2009: Spends six months travelling in India and Nepal.

2013: Exhibits his design for the *Line* coat rack at the Saint-Etienne International Design Biennale Internationale de Design, Saint-Etienne.

Initially trained in industrial design, this imaginative young designer is now interested primarily in eco-design, finding inspiration in objects and their stories. Recycling and combining are the watchwords governing his approach, which he describes as 'ethical and pragmatic'. Moving between art and craftsmanship, his designs are challenging and seductive in their simplicity.

'Designing around the theme of nature carries echoes of the work of contemporary land artists, while at the same time paying homage to the traditional manual skills that our grandparents' generation would have known.

'There's something exhilarating about setting out to design objects or furniture quite simply from natural elements, things that you might have found on a walk in the woods, along the beach or in the countryside.

'But there's always an element of risk, too: you have to understand the materials, to test their durability. You need to know how they will behave when taken out of their natural habitat and placed in a domestic interior. Nature is unforgiving. It's easy to make mistakes, and the materials have to be handled with care, from start to finish. You have to check every step before finally going ahead at each stage, trying out the effects of gluing here or drilling there to make sure the raw materials respond in the way you want.

'The first consideration in a design is the function, followed by the aesthetics. And nature makes it easy to combine the two seamlessly – *Gepetto* brings all the grace of silver birches to a coat stand, *Ambroise* displays bibelots against the subtle monochrome of slate, and *Lumberjack* welcomes visitors with wood in its natural state.

'I enjoy the vision of artists such as Andy Goldsworthy, who use nature to create objects and sculptures that highlight the essence of our natural environment.'

Jean-Marie Reymond

6 *bis*, rue Noire – 44000 Nantes, France
Tel: +33 (0)2 40 48 54 96

behance.net/jdce
behance.net/ruenoire

Left to right: *Lumberjack* (p. 59) ▪ *Ambroise* (p. 17) ▪ *Les Empotés* (p. 97)
Gepetto (p. 77) ▪ *Falling Leaves* (p. 137) ▪ *Vasco* (p. 25)

PÁJARO

A walk in the woods is all you need to bring a little of the natural world
into your interiors. A fallen branch, a length of ribbon,
a decorative touch, and suddenly a child's bedroom takes on a fairytale air.

Pájaro (sparrow in Spanish) is an original and easy-to-make way of hanging clothes
that can fit snugly into the smallest space. And of course it makes a
perfect perch for any feathered friends who happen to be passing through.

DESIGN BY:
AURÉLIE DROUET

STYLING:
ATELIER DU PETIT PARC

PÁJARO

TOOLBOX

Tools

- Spatula knife
- Wire brush
- Handsaw
- Detail sander
- Extra-fine sandpaper
- Bowl and sponge
- Scissors
- 2 hooks + ceiling fixings

Materials

- 1 fallen branch (here from a fir tree) approx. 150cm *(5')* long and 5cm *(2")* in diameter (to fit clothes hanger hooks)
- 4m *(13')* cotton tape (in a colour of your choice)

Telling details: Economy and simplicity combined with practicality and charm.

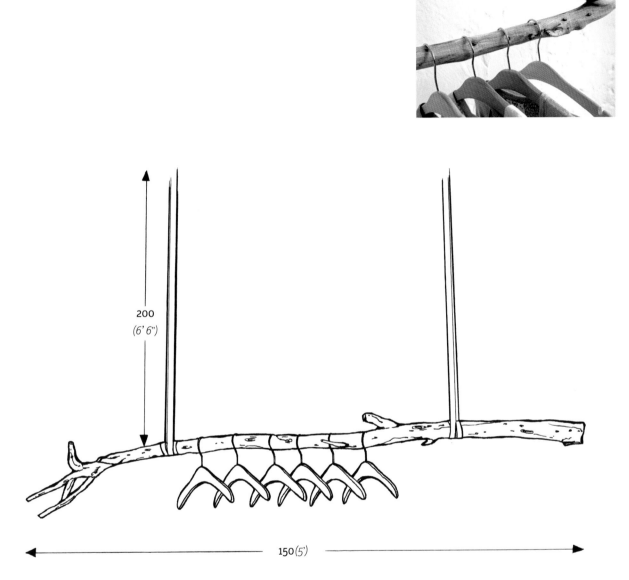

200
(6' 6")

150*(5')*

All measurements are in centimetres and inches (to nearest fraction).

Step-by-step-guide

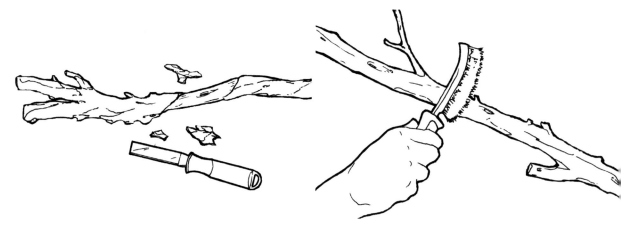

1. Remove the bark with a spatula knife.

2. Clean the branch with a wire brush.

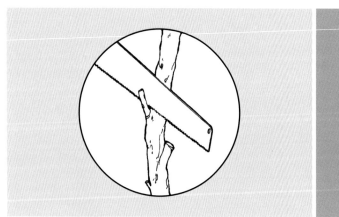

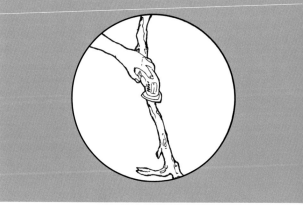

3. Saw off any side branches that you don't want to keep.

4. Sand the branch with a detail sander, finishing hard-to-reach areas by hand. To achieve a smooth surface, finish off with extra-fine sandpaper.

5. Wash the branch with clean water. Take care not to soak it, and leave it to dry for at least 48 hours, either inside or outside in the sun.

6. Cut 2 lengths of tape to twice the depth required to hang the branch plus a bit extra to allow for winding around it. Taking the middle of the length of tape, wind one of the lengths round each end of the branch.

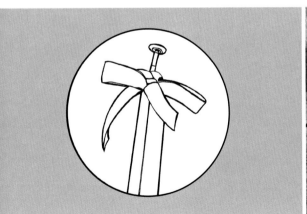

7. Fit the ceiling fixings to the ceiling, screw in the hooks and tie the ends of the tapes to them very firmly.

8. Tape, chain, cord or cable: all are available in a huge range of colours and finishes to coordinate with any interior.

POP'OUF

DESIGN

What could be more inviting or easier to accommodate than a soft wool pouffe?
This mega-crochet pouffe uses a thick pure virgin wool yarn to make it feel even cosier.

Crochet is much easier than you think, and once you've mastered the basics
it's easy to improvise and make up your own designs.

DESIGN BY:
BÉATRICE SIMON (LILLICROCHE)

STYLING:
ANNABEL GUERET (EDMOND)

POP'OUF

TOOLBOX	
Tools	**Materials**
<ul><li>Size 12 crochet hook, size 12</li><li>Scissors</li><li>Large-eye tapestry needle</li><li>Sewing machine + needle + thread</li></ul>	<ul><li>Hessian</li><li>30 x 50g *(1.8oz)* balls of yarn of your choice</li><li>3.5kg *(8lbs)* wool for stuffing, or other stuffing of your choice.</li></ul>

Telling details: Soft wool crocheted on a grand scale offers both style and comfort.

✳ *To start off, follow the
crochet tutorial on pp. 176 and 177
and the diagram on p. 179.*

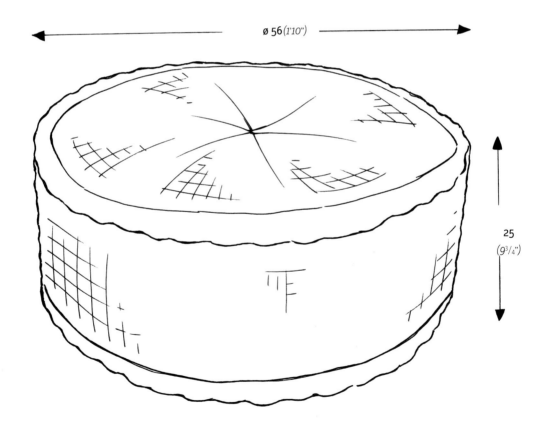

ø 56 *(1'10")*

25
(9³/₄")

All measurements are in centimetres and inches (to nearest fraction).

Step-by-step-guide

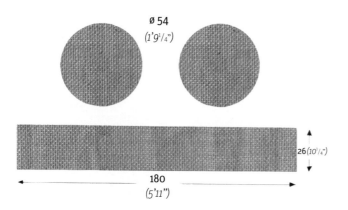

Ø 54
(1'9¹/₄")

26 (10¹/₄")

180
(5'11")

INNER CUSHION

1. Lay the hessian flat and cut out 2 circles of 54cm (1'9¹/₄") diameter and a rectangle of 26 (10¹/₄") x 180cm (5'11") (including seams). Oversew the edges.

2. Fold over 5cm (2") on each of the short edges of the rectangle. Pin together the rectangle and one of the circles, then machine-sew them together 1.5 cm (⁵/₈") in from the edge. Do the same with the other circle. Leave the side of the rectangle open for the stuffing.

3. Turn the right way out and stuff it with wool or other stuffing of your choice. Oversew the seam to close it.

4. To make a firm, plump pouffe, be generous with the stuffing and pack it in firmly.

ABREVIATIONS

ch: chain stitch	dc: double crochet	sl st: slip stitch	tr: treble crochet

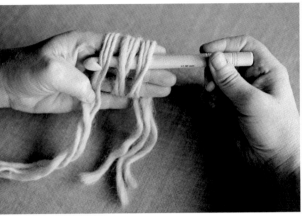

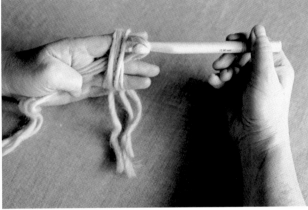

TOP

5. Using a size 12 crochet hook and 3 strands of wool, start by wrapping the strands round your fingers twice to make a centre ring: see tutorial on pp. 176–7.

6. Draw the strands back through the loops.

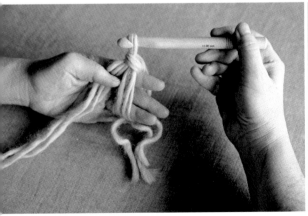

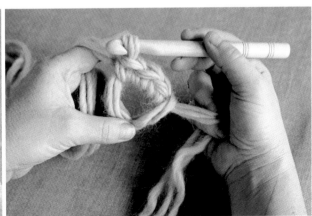

7. Work 1 ch.

8. <u>Row 1:</u> work 6 ch around the centre ring.

Step-by-step-guide

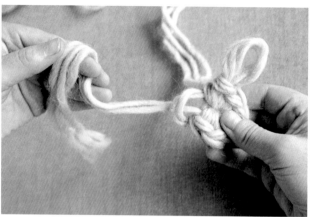

9. Tighten the ring by pulling the strands twice and carry on working in a circle.

10. <u>Row 2:</u> work 2 **dc** in each **ch** of the previous row (= 12 **dc**).

Crochet patterns often have a series of steps that are repeated across a row. Rather than writing these out time after time, asterisks (*) are used to indicate the repeats.

11. <u>Row 3:</u> work * 1 **dc** in the following **dc**, 2 **dc** in the next **dc** *. Repeat 5 times from * to * (row 3 = 18 **dc**). <u>Row 4:</u> work ** 1 **dc** in the 2 next **dc**, 2 **dc** in the next one **. Repeat 5 times from ** to ** (row 4 = 24 **dc**).

12. <u>Rows 5 to 15</u>: continue as for row 4, in each row adding another **dc** to the following **dc** 3–13 (= 90 **dc**). Close the last **dc** row by making a **sl st** in the first **dc** of row 15.
NB: the extra stitches should always be worked on the extra stitches of the previous step.

ABREVIATIONS

| ch: chain stitch | dc: double crochet | sl st: slip stitch | tr: treble crochet |

13. <u>Row 16</u>: popcorn stitch row (top). For the first popcorn stitch, work 3 ch and 3 tr on the same dc of the previous row.

14. Remove the hook from the loop and insert in the third ch.

15. Pick up the loop and bring it back through the third ch.

16. Make a ch, skip a dc and, for the next popcorn stitch, work 4 tr in the next dc.

Step-by-step-guide

17. Remove the hook from the loop, insert it in the top of the first of the 4 **tr** and draw back the loop.

18. Repeat steps 16 and 17 43 times. Finish with 1 **ch** and 1 **sl st** in the centre of the first popcorn stitch in the row (= 45 popcorn stitches alternating with 45 chain stitches).

BOTTOM

19. Repeat steps 5 to 12. Cut the yarn, keeping the end long enough to start sewing the seam.

LA TRANCHE DU POUF

20. **Row 1:** work 1 **ch** and 1 **dc** in the centre of the same popcorn stitch and 1 **dc** by inserting the hook under the following **ch**. Work *** 1 **dc** in the centre of the following popcorn stitch and 1 **dc**, inserting the hook under the following **ch** ***. Repeat 43 times from *** to ***. Finish the row with a **sl st** in the first **dc** of the row.

ABREVIATIONS

ch: chain stitch	**dc:** double crochet	**sl st:** slip stitch	**tr:** treble crochet

21. <u>Row 2</u>: work 1 **ch** and 1 **dc** in the same **dc**, then 1 **dc** in each of the following 89 **dc**. Finish the row with a **sl st** in the first **dc** of the row (= 90 **dc**). Repeat this row 9 times (= 11 rows of **dc**).

22. For the bottom row of popcorn stitch, repeat steps 13 to 18 (= 45 popcorn stitches alternating with 45 chain stitches). Cut the yarn and thread it through the crochet loop before tucking it in.

ASSEMBLING THE POUFFE

23. Put the hessian cushion inside the crocheted cover. Use a tapestry needle to sew the bottom of the cover to the sides, matching the 90 stitches on each side. Tie off any loose ends and tuck them in.

Béatrice Simon
Designer

Béatrice in 5 dates

1990-1997: Worked for the post office in Stuttgart, Germany, every summer – 'an unforgettable human experience'.

2005: Translator.

2006: Publication of first translation of a book on knitting.

2008: First broadcast on German television, presenting a crochet technique from one of her designs.

2009: Returns to France, to her native town near Rennes. Sets up Lillicroche.

A linguist and German scholar by training, Béatrice was a teacher, translator, interpreter and lexicographer before she became a designer – an unusual career path for this passionate crocheter who has done a U-turn in order to create her own designs and publish books on the subject, and who is discreet and generous in sharing her skills with beginners and experienced practitioners alike.

'It seemed completely natural to me to work on designs for this book using natural materials, as these are the materials I prefer to work with on a daily basis, by a long way! Pure wool, locally sourced materials, and as few synthetic materials as possible – except perhaps to lend solidity and structure. The resources we need are never very far away. We just need to keep our eyes and ears open, and visit a few markets and trade shows.

'Making furniture using natural materials fits well with all the other things crochet can be used for – all sorts of accessories of all shapes and sizes. To make a large design, it's best to work with crochet stitches on a similarly mega scale, even if you have to spend hours – or even days – on it, even if it's not a very ergonomic use of your time.

'Natural materials can be more delicate, and also more difficult to look after. But they are part of an authentic philosophy. Their virtues – in terms of ecology, durability and availability – together outweigh any drawbacks they may have.'

Béatrice Simon
lillicroche@yahoo.fr
lillicroche.wordpress.com

Pop'Ouf (p. 41)

ZEPHYR

DESIGN

'I remember how I used to plait the strands of my grandmother's door curtain,
little plastic beads in red, blue, green and yellow.
I remember how I used to love the feeling of walking through it, again and again,
enjoying the noise it made and the way it seemed to caress your skin.
Zephyr, on the other hand, resonates like a gong!'

This bamboo door curtain is a classic revisited,
shedding an unfamiliar light on a familiar material.
It can be made in any size to suit your needs,
and can even – in an extra-large version – be used as a room divider.

DESIGN BY:
MARION DAVIAUD

ZEPHYR

TOOLBOX	
Tools	**Materials**
▪ Radial arm saw with fine blade ▪ Circular saw + wood drill bit (2-3mm $(5/64")$ diameter) ▪ Fine sandpaper ▪ Large sewing needle	▪ Bamboo canes (4cm $(1^1/_2")$ diameter) for the 10 strands of 26 rings ▪ 1 bamboo cane (3.5cm $(1^1/_4")$ diameter) for the pole ▪ 30m $(9'10')$ 12-strand hemp twine, unwaxed ▪ 2 curtain pole brackets (3.5cm $(1^1/_4")$ diameter) ▪ Screws and fixings appropriate for your wall

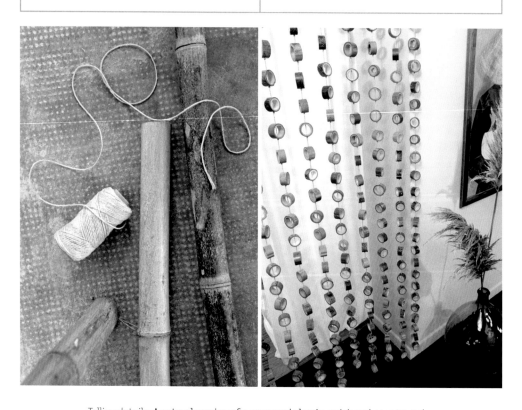

Telling details: A natural version of a seasoned classic, quick and easy to make.

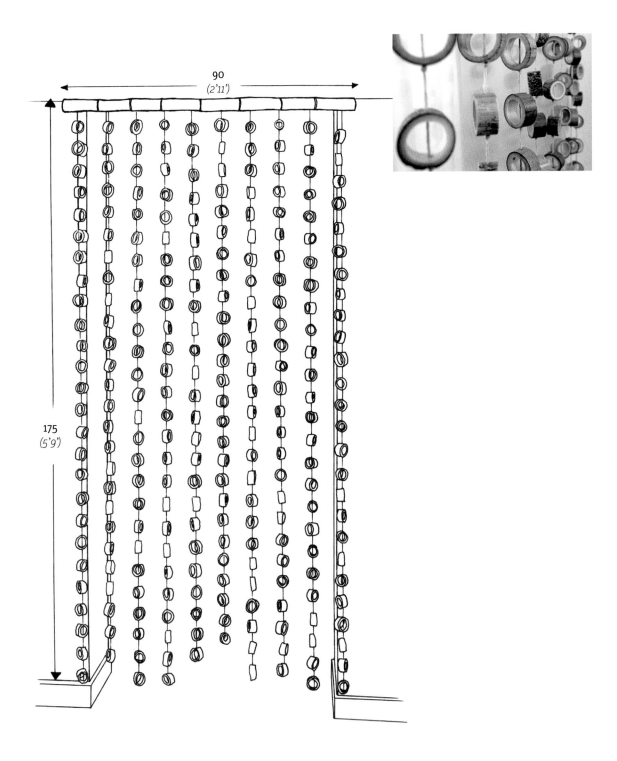

All measurements are in centimetres and inches (to nearest fraction).

Step-by-step-guide

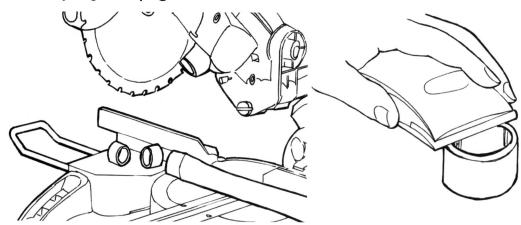

BAMBOO

1. Saw the bamboo cames into 260 2cm(³/₄") sections to make 10 strands, each with 26 rings.

2. Finish the bamboo rings with fine sandpaper.

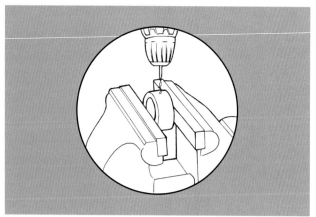

3. Drill holes through both sides of each ring, using a 2-3mm(⁵/₆₄") drill bit.

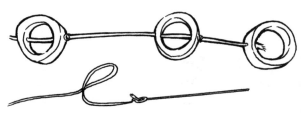

STRANDS

4. Cut a length of twine according to the height of your door frame, allowing an extra margin for the knots (here, 270cm(8'10") for a doorway measuring 175cm(5'9")). Thread a large needle with the twine, and thread the rings bamboo rings on to it, spacing them evenly and making a knot beneath each one.

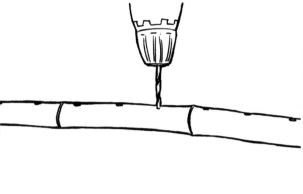

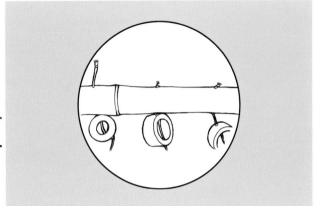

5. Saw the bamboo cane to be used as the pole to the width of the doorway (here 90cm (2'11')), plus a small margin either side, then drill 10 regularly spaced holes (here every 8cm (3')).

6. Tie the strands on to the bamboo pole.

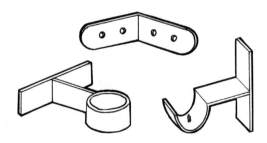

7. Fix brackets to walls or ceiling to suit the position of your curtain.

LUMBERJACK

Sections of tree trunk and a chainsaw*
are all you will need for these hunky, elemental seats.
Sawn from chunks of poplar, *Lumberjack* combines natural and painted wood
finishes to give these uncompromising seats their authentic
and contemporary feel.

*Warning: This design requires the use of a chainsaw.
Chainsaws are potentially dangerous if not used correctly.
It is essential that anyone who uses a chainsaw should have received
adequate training and be competent in its use.

DESIGN BY:
JEAN-MARIE REYMOND

CONSTRUCTION:
JÉRÉMY BOCHE

LUMBERJACK

TOOLBOX	
Tools	**Materials**
▪ Chainsaw	▪ 4 sections of tree trunk (here lime), 40 *(1'3³/₄")* – 50cm *(1'7³/₄")* diameter x 1m *(3'3¹/₂")*
▪ Hammer or mallet	
▪ Wood chisel	▪ Clear exterior wood varnish
▪ Masking tape	▪ Exterior wood paint
▪ Black marker pen	
▪ Belt sander	
▪ Palm sander	
▪ 2 flat paintbrushes	
▪ Sandpaper	

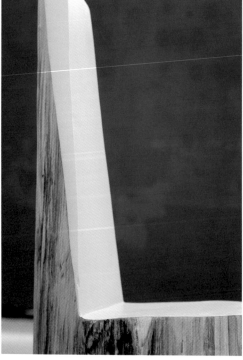

Telling details: Hunky, chunky seats to appeal to your inner lumberjack.

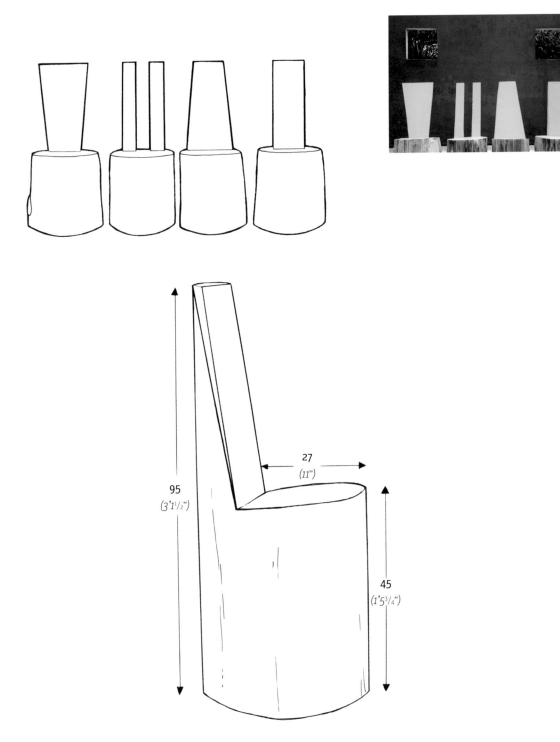

All measurements are in centimetres and inches (to nearest fraction).

Step-by-step-guide

1. Ease off the tree bark using a wood chisel and hammer or mallet, working carefully so as not to damage the wood. Soft woods such as lime are easier to work.

2. Mark the height of the seat, in 3 or places around the circumference, at 47cm (1'6½").

3. Using this mark as a guide, ring the trunk with masking tape at this height.

4. Draw along the masking tape with marker pen to obtain your cutting line.

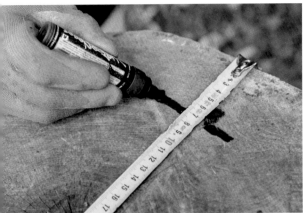

5. Mark the depth of the seat back 7cm(2³/₄")
from the edge.

6. Apply masking tape between this mark
and the cutting line around the circumference,
laying it at a slight angle to create the slope
of the seat back. Draw along this line with
marker pen.

7. Saw down the oblique line of the seat
back. **Safety warning:** Use the chainsaw with
care and proper safety equipment, and always
follow all safety instructions.

8. Following the cutting line, saw through the
diameter of the trunk.

Step-by-step-guide

9. Mark cutting lines for the seat back shape of your choice (see illustrations p. 61) and saw along them.

10. Work slowly and steadily in order to avoid any slips.

11. . Saw the top of the seat back at 50cm (1'7³/₄").

12. Use a belt sander to take the roughness off the sawn surfaces.

13. Use a palm sander with progressively finer sandpapers to obtain a smooth finish.

14. Paint with exterior wood paint.

15. Apply a coat of clear varnish. Allow to dry, then sand very lightly with fine sandpaper. Dust off and apply a second coat.

SUNRISE

Bring a note of the South Seas into your living space with the Sunrise pendant light.
Composed of a cluster of coconut shells,
this exotic chandelier casts an even glow,
ideal for lighting a table.

Playing with contrasting textures,
it combines natural credentials
with a resolutely contemporary design aesthetic.

DESIGN BY:
M&M DESIGNERS

TECHNICAL CONSULTANTS:
FALBALA LUMINAIRES

SUNRISE

TOOLBOX	
<u>Tools</u>	<u>Materials</u>
▪ Hacksaw	▪ 8 coconuts
▪ Knife	▪ 8m *(26')* white fabric lighting cable
▪ Wood drill bit (5mm *(³/₁₆")*)	▪ Strip of 7 5-amp white connectors
▪ Holesaw	▪ 1 15-amp white connector
▪ Cordless drill	▪ 1 clear grommet
▪ Wood file	▪ 7 plain nickel E14 lamp holders
▪ Flat paintbrush	▪ 7 25W G45 E14 mirror bulbs
▪ Small scissors + Retractable knife	▪ Qick-drying PVC or neoprene
▪ Wire strippers	▪ White paint
▪ Electrical screwdriver	▪ 1 Colson collar-type cable tie
▪ Metal drill bits (2mm *(⁵/₆₄")* and 6.5mm *(¹/₄")*)	▪ wood drill bit (5mm *(³/₁₆")*)

Telling details: The rugged contemporary warmth of the coconut fibres and cool vintage sleekness of the fabric cable combine to make a striking and practical design statement

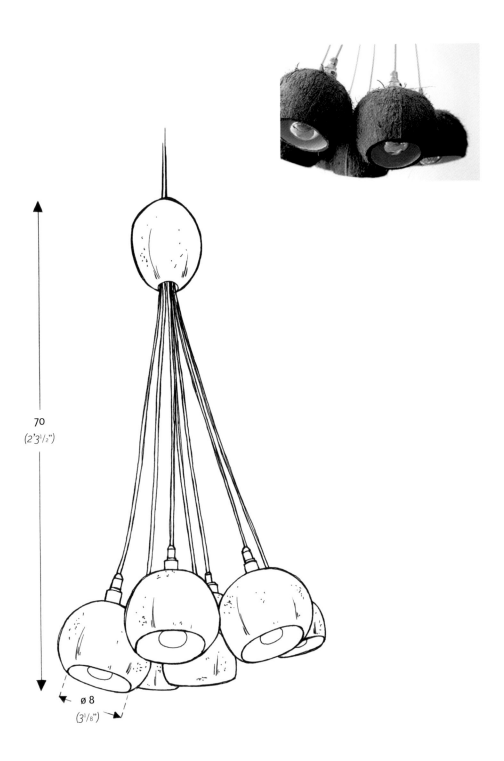

70
(2'3¹/₂")

ø 8
(3¹/₈")

All measurements are in centimetres and inches (to nearest fraction).

Step-by-step-guide

1. With a hacksaw, cut the end (about a quarter) off 7 of the coconut shells.

2. Hollow out the coconut shells with a pointed knife. Wash and allow to dry.

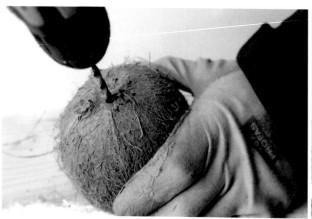

3. Pre-drill the top of each shell using a 5mm (³/₁₆") wood bit.

4. Use a holesaw to drill a hole with a diameter of slightly less than the lamp holder (here 2.5cm (1")).

5. File to adjust the size of the opening to the lamp holder, which should be inserted using gentle pressure.

6. Paint the interior of the shells with two coats of white paint, echoing the white fabric cable.

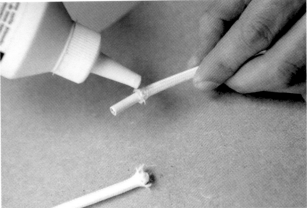

7. Cut the cable into 8 x 1m (3'3") lengths. For the electrical installation, begin by using small scissors to strip the fabric back from the cable for 2cm (³/₄") at each end.

8. To finish off, put a drop of glue on the fabric end, smooth it down and leave to dry. Alternatively, use white electrical tape.

Step-by-step-guide

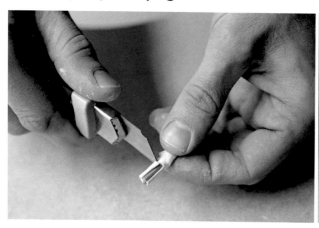

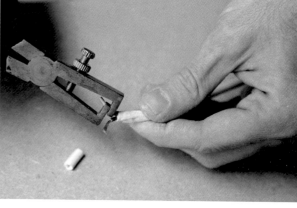

9. Use a retractable knife to strip the cable, cutting through the plastic sheath close to the end of the fabric and taking extra care not cut through the wires.

10. Strip 5mm (³/₁₆") of the wires with the wire strippers, then twist the wires to make the connection easier.

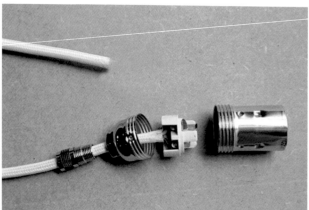

11. Thread the cable into the lamp holder, and connect the wires to the relevant terminals in the lamp holder, grouping them by colour and screwing them in firmly with an electrical screwdriver. Screw the lamp holder together.

12. Screw the lamp holders into the coconut shells, exerting gentle pressure so that they fit snugly.

13. To conceal the connections, take the last coconut shell, cut in half and hollow out, then drill a 2cm(³/₄") hole in one half and a 9.5mm(³/₈") hole in the other. From one of the ends cut off in step 1, cut a ring 2cm(³/₄") wide. Glue this inside the half-shell with the smaller hole.

14. Thread the 7 cables through the half-shell with the larger hole and wire them up to the connector strip, grouping them by colour. Pass 1m(3'3") of the cable through the other half-shell using a clear grommet, then wire it into the connector strip.

15. To prevent the cables from pulling on the connector strip, tie the 7 cables together with a cable tie.

16. Pre-drill through the shell and the ring with a 2mm(⁵/₆₄") metal drill bit, then countersink with a 6.5 mm(¹/₄") drill bit. Screw together using small wood screws, and hang your chandelier from the ceiling.

Sand
Victor Castanera, designer/Barcelona

Areniscos is Victor Castanera's response to the industrial production process and its effects on society, demonstrating the extent to which nature can be a source of creativity, in a process 'combining the senses, durability and aesthetics'.

EACH PIECE IS DELICATELY EXTRACTED FROM THE SAND BY HAND, IN A COMBINATION OF HUMAN SKILLS AND ENVIRONMENTAL FORCES.

CASTANERA WORKS IN SAND DIRECTLY ON THE BEACH, POURING AN ECOLOGICAL ACRYLIC RESIN INTO DEPRESSIONS LEFT BY THE WAVES.

Victor Castanera is a young Spanish designer who views nature as a source for developing new systems and materials of production. For him, 'design is key to changing the world'.

Tel: +34 (0)6 64 35 05 53
castanerav@gmail.com
victorcastanera.com

1. An organic collection of shapes, forms and colours as improvised by the forces of nature.

2. *Areniscos:* every process and every piece is unique.

GEPETTO

Not just a useful coat stand, *Gepetto* is also
a decorative object in its own right,
filling your hallway with the beauty of a grove
of silver birches.

This graphic creation owes its elegance to
the subtle colours and textures of the bark of
this delicate and graceful tree.

DESIGN BY:
JEAN-MARIE REYMOND

GEPETTO

TOOLBOX
<table><tr><td>**Tools** • Cordless drill + 15mm(⁵/₈") wood drill bit • Radial arm saw • Wood file, or rasp • Flat paintbrush • Wood glue</td><td>**Materials** • 3 2.4m(2'10") lengths of 2 x 10cm(4") pine board • 8 1m(3'3") lengths of silver birch branches (approx. 8cm(3") in diameter) • 1m (3'3") length of 16mm(⁵/₈") beech dowelling • Single-thread multi-purpose wood screws • 6 white epoxy L-brackets (5 x 5cm(2")) • White paint</td></tr></table>

Telling details: A useful shelf for keys, post and ornaments and a practical coat stand, all clothed in the delicate monochrome shades and fine textures of silver birch bark.

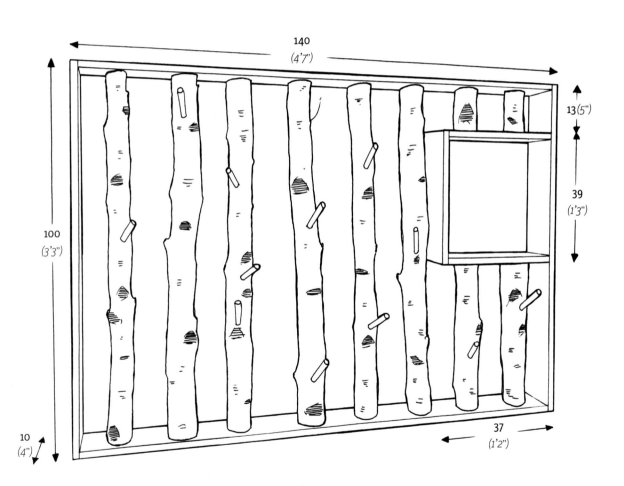

140
(4'7")

13 (5")

39
(1'3")

100
(3'3")

10
(4")

37
(1'2")

All measurements are in centimetres and inches (to nearest fraction).

Step-by-step-guide

1. Saw the pine boards to the following dimensions:
  − 2 lengths of 1.36m *(4'6")* and 2 of 1m *(3'3")* for the main framework,
  − 1 length of 39cm *(1'3")* and 2 of 35cm *(1'1¾")* for the inner framework
Paint one side of each length in white.

2. Assemble the main framework, with the white-painted sides facing inwards and positioning the 1m *(3'3")* lengths outside the 1.36m *(4'6")* lengths. Countersink and pre-drill pilot holes, glue and screw the frame together.

3. Fix the inner frame to the outer frame in the same way.

4. Saw the birch branches to the same length as the inner height of the main frame (here 96cm *(3'2")*). Take care to make straight cuts at both ends in order to create flat surfaces.

5. Position the birch branches to see the effect and work out the distances you need between them.

6. Screw the branches to frame, using 2 or 3 wood screws, attaching the top first and then the bottom.

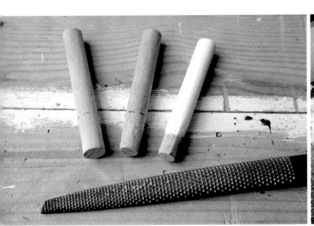

7. Make the coat pegs by sawing 11cm (4¹/₄") lengths of beech dowelling. Taper them over 4cm (1¹/₂") with a file or rasp, then paint them with 2 coats of white paint.

8. Drill each branch with 15mm (⁵/₈") holes, drilling at a slight upward angle and varying them in height and number. Insert the pegs and attach the coat stand to the wall using L-brackets.

梦 *

Imagine an everyday object made from
salvaged odds and ends of wood.

Imagine a piece of furniture that's child's
play to make, with no nails or screws.

Imagine *Dreams*, three bits of wood
put together to make a stylish and
resolutely contemporary bench.

Austere and pared back,
it will look at home both inside and outside.

*'Dream' in Chinese.

DESIGN BY:
MARION DAVIAUD

TOOLBOX

Tools

- Metal square
- Orbital sander
  (with 50, 80 and 120-grit sandpapers)
- Jigsaw
- Mallet
- Flat paintbrush

Materials

- 2 sheets of laminate or other salvaged timber (here 41(1'4") x 41(1'4") x 4cm(1½"))
- 1 length of oak beam (here 105(3'5") x 8.5(3⅜") x 20cm(8"))
- Exterior wood paint

Telling details: The purity of the lines of the this bench is matched by the simplicity of its structure.

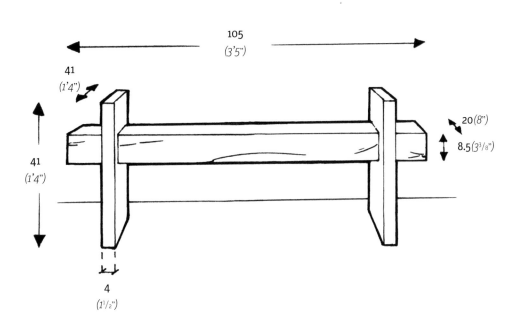

All measurements are in centimetres and inches (to nearest fraction).

Step-by-step-guide

1. Sand the oak beam with an orbital sander. Begin with the 50-grit sandpaper and finish with the 120-grit for a perfectly smooth finish.

2. Measure the width and depth of the beam.

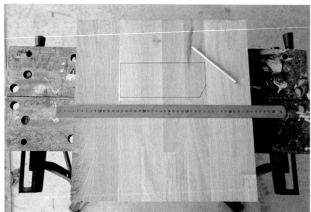

3. Mark these measurements on the square sheets of laminate or other salvaged timber, placing them centrally on their width and keeping them equidistant from the sides and top edge.

4. To saw the holes, drill 2 or 3 holes slightly larger in diameter than the jigsaw blade in each corner against the cutting line.

5. Insert the jigsaw blade in the holes and saw carefully along the marked line. Sand the holes and the bench sides.

6. To assemble the bench, use a mallet and wood chock and tap the sides gently but firmly into position.

7. To highlight the lines of the bench, paint the sides but not the seat. The combination of plain white and natural wood lends the bench its contemporary look.

8. <u>Option</u>: To protect the seat from fading while preserving its appearance, you can if you wish treat it with a mixture of equal parts of linseed oil and turpentine.

Marion Daviaud
Designer

Marion in 6 dates

2005: Graduates in merchandise design from CEPRECO, Lille.

2008: Sets up her own business, Le Fourbi créatif de Macha.

2009: Moves to a new region of France to start a new life with new projects closer to her aspirations.

2010: Carries out the eco-refurbishment of an old house for herself.

2011: Launches a second career teaching the design of commercial spaces.

2012: Birth of her daughter.

Trained in visual merchandising, Marion gradually turned her back on this field in order to concentrate on craft and design, crowning her efforts with the establishment of her own business in 2008. From salvage and reclamation, her approach evolved towards the eco-design work that has become her signature style. Giving pride of place to natural and organic materials, recycling and locally sourced skills, Marion focuses on creating unique pieces and working to commission. Since 2011, she has combined this philosophy of design with teaching the design of commercial spaces.

'Nature is an inexhaustible source of inspiration, as it offers such a wealth of forms, materials, colours and even concepts! The creative potential is limitless, as it is so vast in scale and varied in scope. Nature is all around us and within us, ubiquitous and omnipresent.

'Designing with natural materials invites you to work instinctively, with your senses. Some materials can be unpredictable or uncontrollable. Their irregularities, which give them their charm, can make them difficult to work with. So you have to adapt, while at the same time being careful to preserve the material's essence and qualities. Most of these materials are 'naturally' beautiful, and offer fascinating textures. They give an object its soul.

'You can also take inspiration from natural forms, as I did with the Organic light, in a design that symbolizes the living world in simple forms.'

Marion Daviaud

6, rue des Pêcheurs – 44140 Remouillé, France
Tel: +33 (0)2 40 06 62 56

contact@lefourbicreatif.com
lefourbicreatif.com

ALOHA

The traditional coat stand — long out of favour — is now gracing our hallways with a
contemporary spin, thanks to the new generation of designers.
Combining practicality with aesthetics,
Aloha is easy to make and requires nothing more than
some bamboo canes and coir twine.

The minimalist construction of this eco-design
is in complete harmony with the philosophy that underlies it,
and its unassuming simplicity is a tribute to the beauty of natural materials.

DESIGN BY:
M&M DESIGNERS

ALOHA

TOOLBOX	
Tools	**Materials**
▪ Radial arm saw or hacksaw ▪ Sanding block + fine sandpaper ▪ Retractable knife ▪ Cordless drill	▪ 5 bamboo canes, around 3m(9'10") long and 4(1¹/₂")–6cm(2") in diameter ▪ 50m(16') x 4mm(⁵/₃₂") brown coir twine ▪ 4 lengths of flat batten at least 80cm(2'8") long ▪ Wood screws ▪ Wood glue ▪ Wide masking tape ▪ Electrical tape

Telling details: Contrasting natural textures and a minimalist use of materials combine to make a design in which all the elements are in easy and natural harmony.

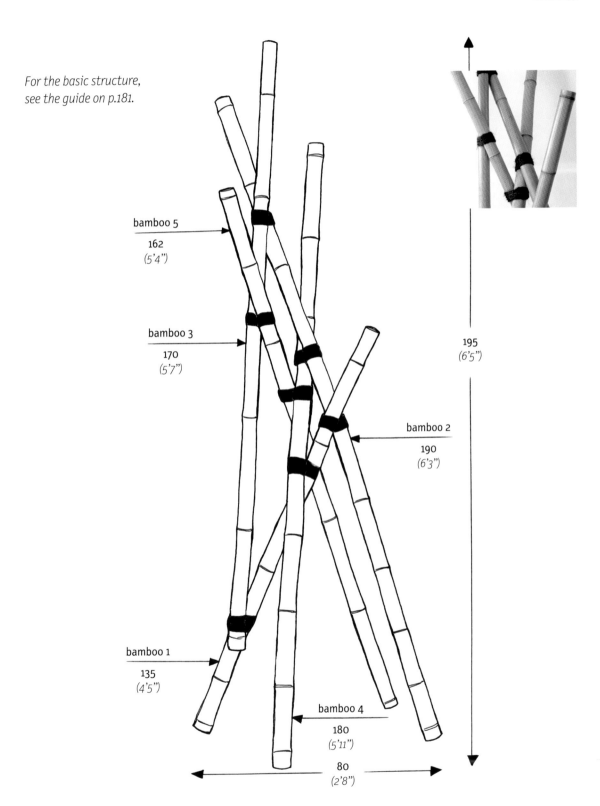

*For the basic structure,
see the guide on p.181.*

bamboo 5
162
(5'4")

bamboo 3
170
(5'7")

bamboo 2
190
(6'3")

195
(6'5")

bamboo 1
135
(4'5")

bamboo 4
180
(5'11")

80
(2'8")

All measurements are in centimetres and inches (to nearest fraction).

Step-by-step-guide

1.

2.

1. Cut the bamboo canes to the following lengths:
n°1 = 135 cm (4'5")
n°2 = 190 cm (6'3")
n°3 = 170 cm (5'7")
n°4 = 180 cm (5'11")
n°5 = 162 cm (5'4")
Cut above a knot and put tape round the section to be cut in order to avoid any splintering.

2. Lightly sand the sawn ends.

3.

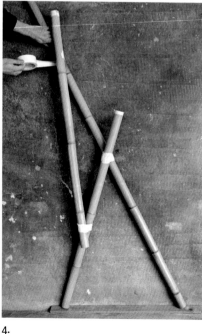

4.

3. Make the templates for the basic structure (1 flat batten), then the whole structure (2 flat battens forming a cross):
▪ 1 80cm (2'8") flat batten with 2 screws 60cm (2') apart,
▪ 1 cross with 2 screws per 80cm (2'8") flat batten, placed 60cm (2') apart, to correspond to the legs.

4. Wedge the template for the basic structure against a wall, then lay out the first 3 bamboo canes on the floor, no 1 resting on n° 2, and n° 3 resting on both of them, then tape them together (cf. see the diagram on p.181).

4. Position the basic structure on the cross-shaped template.
Position cane n°4 to support n°s1 and 2, and cane n°5 on n°s3 and 4, inside the triangle formed at step 4.
Tape the canes together as you go.

5. Remove the tape from one of the intersecting points between 2 canes and put a spot of wood glue between them. Cut a length of around 2m(6'7") of twine, tape the ends to stop them fraying, spread glue over 5cm(2") at one end, wedge this into the joint and wind the twine several times around the 2 canes until it is all used.

5.

6.

7. Finish off by tucking the twine inside and pulling it tight.

8. Cut the cord as short as possible with a retractable knife, and squirt wood glue between the twine and the cane. Wipe off any surplus with a cloth.

7.

8.

LES EMPOTÉS

DESIGN

Bring nature into your living space.

Transform a superannuated coffee table into a miniature indoor garden,
or festoon an old chair with greenery. Spectacular orchids, delicate ferns, architectural succulents:
plants and furniture together bring beauty, fragrance and a whole new dimension.

DESIGN BY:
JEAN-MARIE REYMOND

LES EMPOTÉS

TOOLBOX

Tools

- Ruler and carpenter's pencil
- Jigsaw
- Drill
- Orbital sander
- 1 small paint roller, 1 flat paintbrush
  and 1 sash brush

Materials

- Old furniture
  (e.g. table, bedside cabinet, chair)
- Planters of any shape or size to fit
- Pot plants of your choice
- Multi-purpose compost and clay pebbles
- Paint in the colour of your choice
- Clear matt water-resistant varnish

Telling details: Customize furniture that has seen better days with plants to give it a new lease of life
and create unique indoor plantings.

40
(1'3")

8(2'7")

46(1'6")

130(4'3")

42 (1'4")

59(1'11")

43 (1'5")

60(2')

27(11')

20(8")

20(8")

15(6")

15(6")

25(10")

15(6")

All measurements are in centimetres and inches (to nearest fraction).

Step-by-step-guide

1. Position your pot on your piece of furniture and trace its outline.

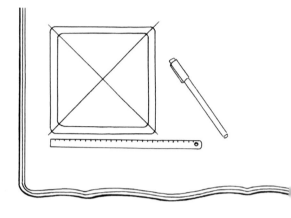

2. To create a smaller opening to secure the pot in place, draw a second line 5mm (³/₁₆") inside the first.

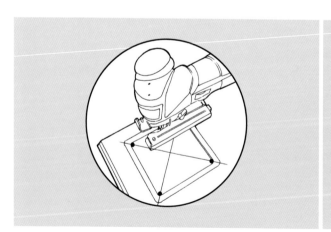

3. To saw the opening, draw holes slightly larger than your jigsaw blade inside the second line and in the corners. Insert the jigsaw blade in the holes and saw carefully.

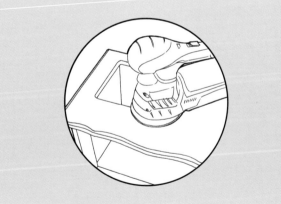

4. Sand the flat surfaces with an orbital sander, and sand the more difficult areas (legs, mouldings, grooves etc.) by hand.

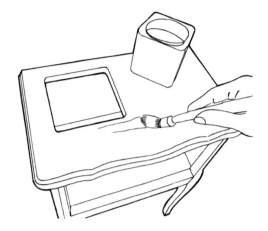

5. Paint the furniture in a fresh colour to set off your plants.

6. Apply 2 coats of clear matt water-resistant varnish. This will enable you to water the plants without damaging the furniture.

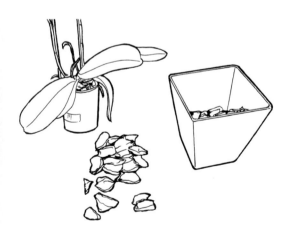

7. To ensure your plants grow well, follow the growing instructions when potting them up.

ORGANIC

Inspired by mapping contours,
the *Organic* pendant light symbolizes nature through its form rather than its materials.
The movement of the land, as conveyed by geographical relief, here shapes an object to hang in the air,
where it spreads a nimbus of softly filtered light.
Perfect for a child's bedroom, *Organic* will look equally stylish in a living room.

DESIGN BY:
MARION DAVIAUD

TECHNICAL CONSULTANTS:
FALBALA LUMINAIRES

ORGANIC

TOOLBOX	
Tools	**Materials**

▪ Jigsaw
▪ Cordless drill
  (with 9 $(^{11}/_{32})$ and 16mm $(^5/_8")$ wood drill)
▪ Sanding block + fine sandpaper
▪ Spatula
▪ Gimlet
▪ Flat spanners
▪ Wire cutters
▪ Small paint roller
	▪ 5 sheets MDF $(70 (2'3^1/_2")$ x $110 (2'3^1/_2")$ x 2cm $(^3/_4"))$
	▪ 1m $(3'3")$ threaded rod (8mm $(^5/_{16}")$ diameter)
	▪ 30 x 8mm $(^5/_{16}")$ nuts
	▪ Hooks (3 medium for the MDF,
	  3 large for the ceiling)
	▪ Wood filler + white paint
	▪ 6 wire rope thimbles + 6 wire rope clamps
	▪ 3m $(9'10")$ steel cable
	  (adjust according to your needs)
	▪ 1 white lamp holder
	▪ 1 10W E27 low energy light bulb

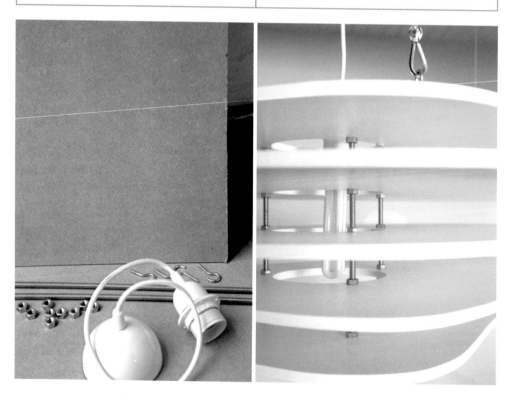

Telling details: Softly curving tiers shed a nimbus of filtered light.

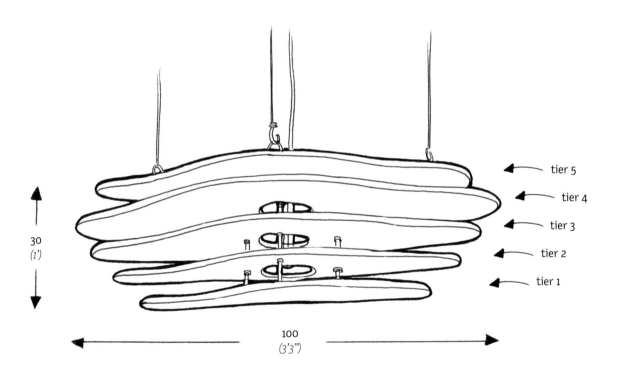

tier 5

tier 4

tier 3

tier 2

tier 1

30
(1')

100
(3'3")

All measurements are in centimetres and inches (to nearest fraction).

Step-by-step-guide

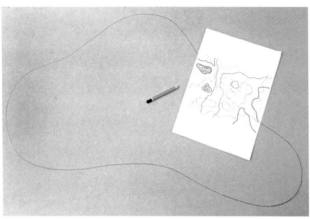

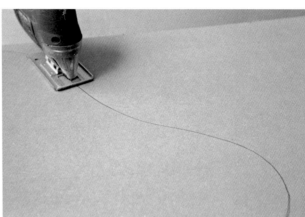

1. Using a contour map for inspiration, draw your desired shape for the first tier of the light on the first sheet of MDF.

2. Saw round tier 1, then use it as a template for the same shape but slightly larger for tier 2, tracing the outline freehand.

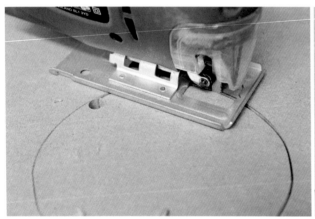

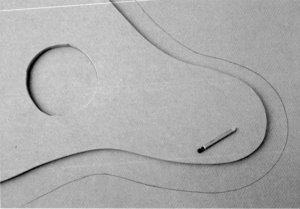

3. Draw a circle of 14cm (5½") diameter in the centre of tier 2. Just inside the line, drill a hole of a diameter slightly larger than your jigsaw blade. Insert the blade in the hole and saw round the circle.

4. Cut 2 more versions of tier 2, each slightly larger than the one before, to make tiers 4 and 5, and a third exactly the same as tier 2 to make tier 5.

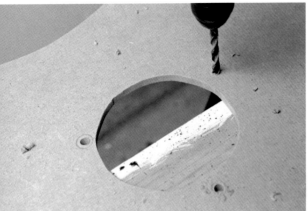

5. Drill 3 holes using 9mm(¹¹/₃₂) wood bit around the circular opening in tiers 2 to 5, to pass the threaded steel rods through.

6. Transfer the positions of these 3 holes on to the side of tier 1 that will show. Using a 16mm(⁵/₈") wood bit, drill blind holes 8mm(⁵/₁₆") deep (the depth of the nuts), then drill 9mm(¹¹/₃₂) holes for the threaded steel rods in the centre.

7. Sand and paint all the tiers, except for the visible side of tier 1, where you will need to conceal the nuts with wood filler.

8. Saw the threaded steel rod into 3 lengths of 26cm(10¹/₄"), being careful to leave a clean edge.

Step-by-step-guide

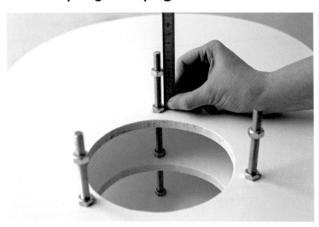

9. Thread the tiers on to the steel rods, leaving 5cm *(2")* between each tier and the next.

10. Screw the nuts on tightly.

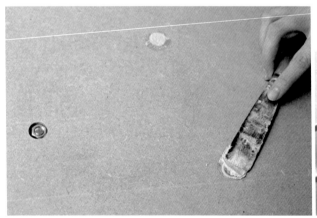

11. To conceal the nuts, use a spatula to fill the holes with wood filler, smooth off the surface and allow to dry.

12. Sand the wood filler lightly with fine sandpaper, then apply 2 coats of paint.

13. Cut the steel cable into 3 equal lengths, then attach a rope thimble and clamp at each end.

14. Use a gimlet to prepare holes in tier 5, then screw in the 3 hanging hooks.

15. The lamp holder and lampshade are hung separately. Screw hanging hooks into the ceiling, screw in the hooks and hang the cables from them.

Rattan
Métalobil, Design agency / Nantes

The Métalobil design agency excels in working with rattan, mastering the properties of this natural fibre with such skill that they are able to create unique installations combining design excellence with technical virtuosity. Their skills are constantly evolving, creating poetic, plastic pieces that offer a fresh vision of our environment.

FIBRILLES PUBLIC BENCHES, MADE FROM LENGTHS OF RATTAN, INVITE SHOPPERS AT THE BEAULIEU SHOPPING MALL IN NANTES TO PAUSE FOR A MOMENT.

STRIPPED AND PARTLY DYED RATTAN CLOTHES AN 'ORGANIC' STAIRCASE DESIGN BY THE TETRARC ARCHITECTURE AGENCY (MAISON DES ARTS DE SAINT-HERBLAIN).

Started in 2004 by the architect Matthieu Lebot and the artist and sculptor Freddy Bernard, the Métalobil agency offers rigorous technical skills combined with a distinctive artistic inspiration, drawing on the fields of engineering design, stage design, furniture design and one-off installations.

Métalobil
ZA Champ Fleuri
15 rue des Coquelicots – 44840 Les Sorinières, France
Tél.: +33 (0)2 40 69 56 03
clic@metalobil.fr – metalobil.fr

1

1. The *Petit salon d'écoute* (Little Listening Room), designed for the Lieu Unique in Nantes, stretches and changes shape to mould itself to the space it sits in and to the human body.

2

2.. Curves, layers and colours make rattan an eye-catching design material.

BURNT OFFERING

DESIGN

Burnt Offering offers a fresh twist
on a time-honoured classic in
the decorative repertoire, wood.
The deep black scorched outer surface of
the wood contrasts strongly with the silvery
white of the tapered surfaces
of the natural wood.

Fire is here used as a natural treatment
to obtain a specific look, the intensity of
the flame and the type of wood offering a range
of different effects, from light scorched brown
to intense velvety black.

DESIGN BY:
M&M DESIGNERS

STYLING:
ANNABEL GUERET *(EDMOND)*

BURNT OFFERING

TOOLBOX

Tools

- Radial arm saw
- Cordless drill
- 2.5cm (1") flat wood drill bit
- 7mm (17/64") wood drill bit
- Small gas blow torch
- Flat paintbrush

Materials

- 1 x 160cm (5'3") chestnut stake (5cm (2") diameter)
- Clear matt varnish
- 3cm dowels (6mm (5/64") diameter)
- Pink paint marker pen
- Black paint

Cluster:

- 1 x 150cm (4' 11") length of silver birch trunk (5-8cm (2"-3") diameter)
- 4 x 10cm (4") flat-bottomed tubular glass vases (here 2.4cm (1") diameter)

Telling details: A design of infinite possibilities – of different heights and the number of candles or vases – that plays on the graphic contrast between natural and scorched wood.

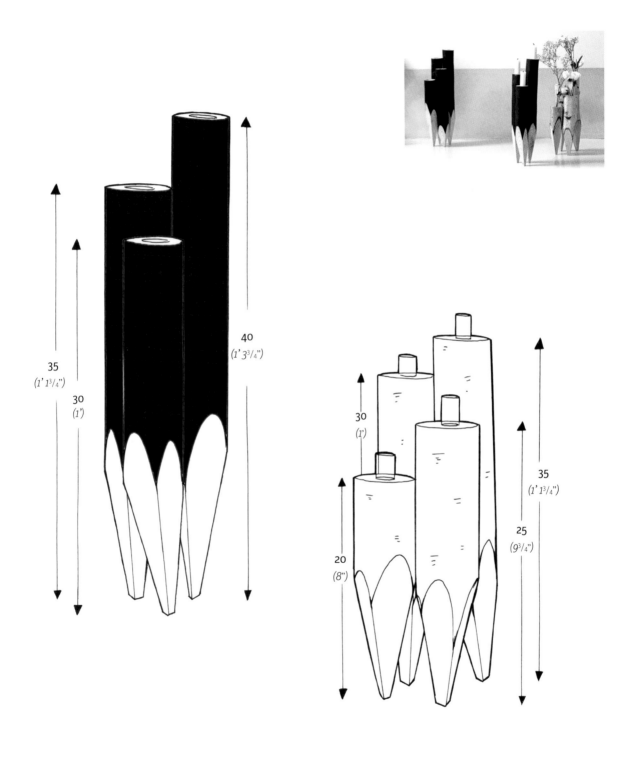

35
(1' 1³/₄")

30
(1')

40
(1' 3³/₄")

30
(1')

20
(8")

35
(1' 1³/₄")

25
(9³/₄")

All measurements are in centimetres and inches (to nearest fraction).

Step-by-step-guide

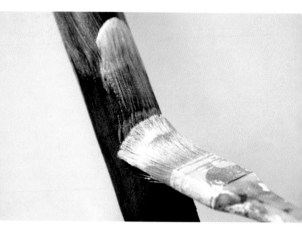

1. Scorch the outer surface of the chestnut stake, holding the blow torch 2-3cm (1-1¹/₂") from the surface and moving it up and down.

2. Apply 2 coats of clear matt varnish.

3. Saw the stake into 3 x 50cm (1'7¹/₄") sections using a radial arm saw.

4. Taper each stake. To saw 4 sides, start with the first side, turn the stake through a quarter-turn to saw the second, and repeat for the third and fourth. Then saw the stakes into 30 (1'), 35 (1'1³/₄")) and 40cm (1'3³/₄") lengths.

5. Drill an off-centre hole into the top of each stake (positioning the centre of the hole 1.8cm(³/₄") from the nearest edge), 4cm(1¹/₂") deep and 2.5cm(1") in diameter. Use tape to mark the desired depth on the drill bit.

6. Mark the points at which the stakes touch, then draw a line from these points down the length of the stake to mark the positions of the dowels. Paint the dowels black.

7. Using a 7mm(¹⁷/₆₄") wood bit, drill 2 holes in the first stake along the line drawn in step 6. Outline the holes with the paint marker pen, then position the second stake on them carefully and press to transfer the paint marks. Drill and insert the dowels. Repeat with the third stake.

8. Variation:
The vase version in birch is made following the same method except for the size of the holes, which measure 7cm(2³/₄") deep and 2.5cm(1") in diameter to hold the tubular glass vases.

BAMBOUSERAIE

DESIGN

Familiar as a graceful ornamental plant in our gardens, bamboo —
widely used in Asian countries for scaffolding and water pipes in construction projects,
as well as for a host of everyday items such as plates and furniture —
has also become increasingly popular with interior designers in recent years.

The *Bambouseraie* stool pays tribute to the versatility and beauty
of the largest, tree-like member of the grass family.

DESIGN BY:
MARION DAVIAUD

CUSHION DESIGN BY:
LES COUSETTES DE NANTES

BAMBOUSERAIE

TOOLBOX	
Tools	**Materials**
<ul><li>Keyhole saw + radial arm saw</li><li>Pillar drill + 2mm *(⁵/₆₄")* wood bit</li><li>Small hammer</li><li>Sewing machine + zipper foot</li><li>Needles, pins, thread, thimble</li><li>Carpenter's pencil or chalk</li><li>Ruler</li><li>Paintbrush</li><li>2 ratchet straps</li></ul>	<ul><li>10 x 250cm *(8'2¹/₂")* bamboo canes</li><li>Plywood cable drum (36cm *(1'2")* high x 50cm *(1'7¹/₄")* diameter)</li><li>Nails</li><li>Wood glue</li><li>5m *(16')* hemp webbing (27cm *(11")* wide)</li><li>5m *(16')* hemp fabric (150cm *(4'11")* wide)</li><li>Jersey fabric: 2 x 60cm *(2')* squares</li><li>2 shank buttons</li><li>200cm *(6' 6")* cord and bias binding</li><li>Feather stuffing from an old pillow</li></ul>

Telling details: Hemp makes an ideal material for a discreet but comfortable cushion
to complement the many natural shades of the bamboo.

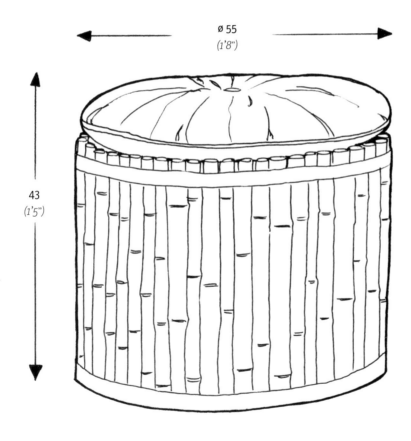

ø 55
(1'8")

43
(1'5")

All measurements are in centimetres and inches (to nearest fraction).

Step-by-step-guide

STRUCTURE

1. Prepare the bamboo canes by cutting off any side-branches with a keyhole saw. Calculate the length to cut them to by measuring the external height of the cable drum and adding 2cm (3/4").

2. Using a radial arm saw, cut the 10 canes to the desired length, then lightly sand both ends.

3. Mark the ends of each cane where it meets the plywood to ensure that the nails go into the ply.

4. Using a pillar drill with a 2mm (5/64") bit, pre-drill pilot holes in the bamboo canes, taking care to go through both sides.

5. Using a small hammer and very fine nails that are longer than the diameter of the bamboo, nail the canes in position. Hammering lightly to avoid splitting the bamboo, nail the bottom of the first bamboo cane, then use a set square to check that it is vertical before nailing the top.

6. Continue with the rest of the canes, starting at the bottom, adjusting, and then nailing the top.

7. Cut 2 lengths of hemp webbing to the same length as the diameter of the cable drum, then spread them with wood glue.

8. Position each length of webbing to cover the nails and glue in place.

Step-by-step-guide

9. Place a ratchet strap around each length of glued webbing and pull tight while the glue dries.

10. To finish, push screwed up newspaper into the end of each cane and cover with wood filler. Smooth off and allow to dry.

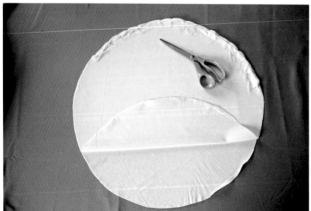

JERSEY INNER CUSHION

11. Cut 2 circles of jersey fabric 57cm *(1'10")* in diameter (the diameter of the stool + 1cm*(³/₈")* seam allowance), place them right sides together, then sew them together with a zigzag 1cm in from the edge. Leave a 15cm *(6")* opening for the stuffing.

12. Turn the right way out and stuff with feathers or other stuffing, then slip stitch the opening.

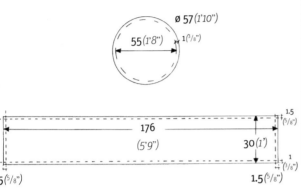

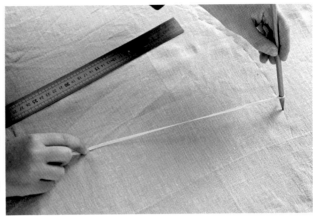

HEMP CUSHION COVER:

13. Wash and iron the hemp fabric. Draw the pattern pieces above and cut round them. Note that the measurements are dictated by the diameter of the stool (here 55cm (1'8")).

14. To draw a circle, take a thread and tie it to a pencil or piece of chalk. Cut the free end to the same length as the cushion radius (here 28.5cm). Hold the free end and use the crayon or chalk like a pair of compasses to draw the circle.

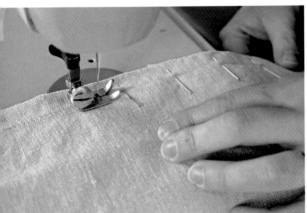

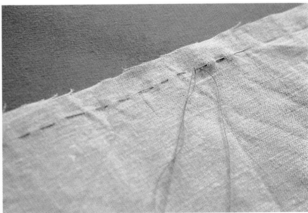

15. Fold the rectangle in 2 lengthwise and sew along both ends, 1.5cm (⁵/₈") in from the edge, to make a tube.

16. To make the gathers, sew along the top of the tube in running stitch, 1.5cm (⁵/₈") in from the edge.

Step-by-step-guide

17. Gather the fabric along the thread and even out the gathers. Knot the thread together, then turn the fabric the other way out.

18. Using a zipper foot, start assembling the piping by stitching the binding to the right side of the tube, keeping the raw edges together.

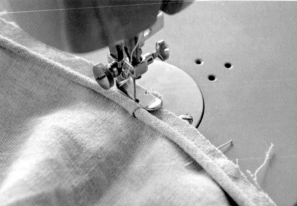

19. To join the piping, cut back 2cm(³/₄") of the bias binding on one side, retaining the cord. Do the same thing in reverse on the other side, cutting back 2cm(³/₄") of cord and retaining the bias binding. Put the ends of the cord together and sew the bias binding together.

20. Sew the piping down.

21. Sew the piping to the circle, right sides facing, leaving a 20cm(8") opening. Turn the right way out.

22. Insert the inner cushion into the cover, then slip stitch to close.

23. Cut a circle of hemp fabric twice the diameter of the button. Sew around it in running stitch, 5mm(³/₁₆") in from the edge, gather on to the button and tie off the thread.

24. Use a long needle to sew on the 2 buttons, starting from underneath and sewing through the cushion from one side to the other. Draw the buttons together with a slip knot, then make 2 or 3 more knots and cut the thread.

Les Cousettes de Nantes
Designers

Les Cousettes in 5 dates

2010: Julia and Tiphaine first meet.

2012: They set up Les Cousettes de Nantes.

2012: First educational support/design of Léo Lagrange costume parade.

2013: First course: 'Making a jacket'.

2013: First stage design, with the Dix collective, for Les Buttineries de Sainte-Anne.

One is a costume designer, the other an interior designer and visual artist. Between them, Julia and Tiphaine work in every field of the performing arts, notably in cinema. For them, these are fields that 'create a relationship with the materials used, whether raw or worked, and constantly feed the senses'. In 2012 they set up the collective Les Cousettes de Nantes in order to share their skills.

'From the outset, the collective's approach has always been to respect and enhance manual skills through sewing and interior decoration. We offer workshops in sewing, courses in different subjects, educational support, and creative, artistic and collective projects in costume and stage design.

'The collective works primarily with reclaimed and natural materials. For the cushion to complement the Bamboustool we chose hemp, the strongest plant fibre in nature, because it doesn't lose its shape or shrink when washed. It has natural anti-bacterial and anti-fungal qualities, so is ideal for everyday use. And its raw appearance and neutral colour go with everything. So it was the obvious choice.'

Les Cousettes de Nantes
cousettes44@gmail.com
lescousettesdenantes.overblog.com

LOOM

Give a new lease of life to a child's chair and transform it into something unique and original.

With its soft and comfortable seat and back threaded with cotton twine, *Loom* is an easy way of personalizing a chair and introducing a discreetly natural note into your interior spaces.

DESIGN BY:
MARION DAVIAUD

STYLING BY:
ATELIER DU PETIT PARC

LOOM

TOOLBOX

Tools

- Drill (or a power multi-tool)
- Detail sander
- Sanding block + fine sandpaper

Materials

- Vintage child's chair
- 10m *(33')* cotton twine
  in the colour of your choice
- Cotton wick
- Beeswax
- Polishing glove

Telling details: Simple, economic and quick to do:
the perfect combination of reclamation and natural materials.

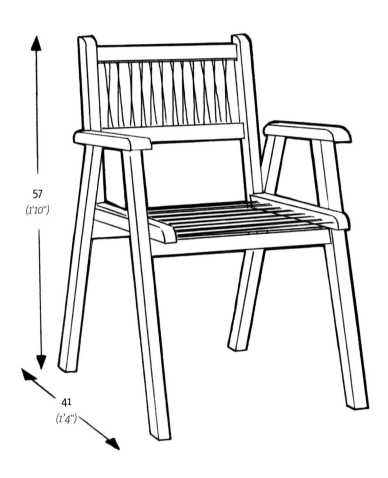

57
(1'10")

41
(1'4")

All measurements are in centimetres and inches (to nearest fraction).

Step-by-step-guide

1. Remove the chair back and seat, then sand the frame.

2. Mark the positions of the holes every 1cm (³/₈").

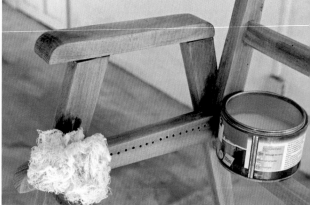

3. Using a small power multi-tool, drill the holes. For delicate work this sort of tool is ideal. A classic drill may also be used but only with great care.

4. Apply beeswax to the whole frame with cotton wick and allow to dry.

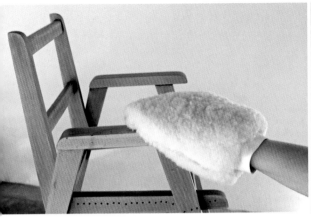

5. Polish the chair using a polishing glove.

6. Thread the cotton twine through the holes, pulling it tight on both the back and the seat.

7. Finish with a knot.

FALLING LEAVES

DESIGN

When the leaves start to fall,
turning every shade of scarlet and gold and dancing
and fluttering on the autumn breeze,
they offer a free natural resource for a range of graphic designs for our walls,
in an original interpretation of classic botanical prints.

Imagination and a range of simple techniques – collage or stencilling,
découpage or painting – are all you need to turn a walk in the woods into images
to brighten your living spaces through the dark winter days.

DESIGN BY:
JEAN-MARIE REYMOND

FALLING LEAVES

TOOLBOX

Tools

- Long ruler + pencil + eraser
- Pair of compasses
- Fine black felt-tip pen
- 2 small paintbrushes
- Bowl
- Kitchen paper
- Cordless drill

Materials

- Assortment of leaves
- 2 sheets of 240gsm cartridge paper (A1)
- Blu-Tack
- 1 52 x 52cm (1'8¹/₄") frame
- 2 27 x 27cm (11') frames
- Glossy glue
- Paint: 3 colours of your choice

Telling details: An original and imaginative take on the classic decorative trope of botanical prints, using real leaves to create cheerful and evocative images.

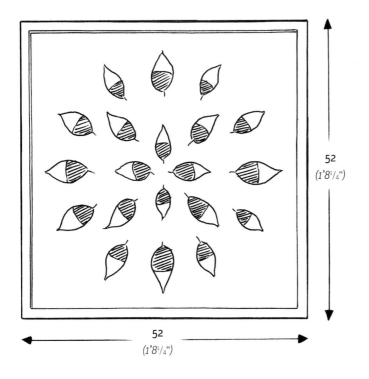

52
(1'8¹/₄")

52
(1'8¹/₄")

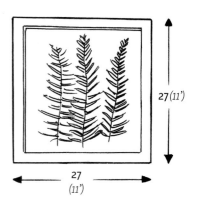

27 (11')

27
(11')

All measurements are in centimetres and inches (to nearest fraction).

Step-by-step-guide

1. Wash the leaves in a bowl of water and dry them gently with kitchen towel, then press them between the pages of a heavy book to flatten them.

2. Cut a 50 x 50cm (1'7¼") square from a sheet of cartridge paper. Lightly sketch in the positions of the leaves (you will rub them out at a later stage): divide the square in 4, add the diagonals, then with a pair of compasses draw 3 circles with radii of 6 (2³/₈"), 11 (4³/₈") and 18cm (7¹/₈").

3. Create your composition by positioning the leaves and fixing them in place with Blu-Tack. Use a fine black felt-tip pen to draw the line of the circle on each leaf, to mark off the sections to be painted.

4. Paint these sections of the leaves with 2 coats of paint in the colours of your choice.

5. Spread the back of the leaves with glossy glue. Rub out the pencil lines around their positions on the cartridge paper, then carefully stick the leaves down. Allow to dry.

6. When all the leaves are glued, rub out all the crayon lines.

7. Apply a coat of glossy glue to all the leaves.

8. Give free rein to your imagination and play with the shapes and colours of the leaves to invent your own gallery of leaf pictures.

Straw
Tété Knecht, designer

It was while she was doing her master's degree at the Ecole Cantonale d'Art in Lausanne that Tété Knecht saw her Paille (Straw) project emerge from a series of experiments in combining different materials. During her researches into materials, their appearance and they way they moved, she produced a marriage of straw and latex, so creating a new material and transforming the objects she made with it.

LAYERS OF STRAW AND LATEX ARE PLACED IN A MOULD UNTIL THEY FORM A THICK SKIN. THE SKINS ARE THEN REMOVED FROM THE MOULDS AND ASSEMBLED TO MAKE A SEAT.

THE PAILLE PROJECT IS 'THE MANIFESTATION OF A CREATIVE PROCESS THAT USES THE HANDS, EYES, AND SENSES. ITS FORM COMES FROM THIS PROCESS. IT IS THE ORIGIN OF ITS CONCEPTION.'

Born in São Paulo, Tété Knecht has lived and worked in Lausanne since 2005. Following a collaboration with the Campana brothers in 2000, she focused her work on recycling scrap materials before concentrating on experimenting with materials, her true passion and signature activity.

ttknecht@bluewin.ch
teteknecht.com

1

1. October 2010: First performance at the Galerie Slott in Paris, a live creation of *Sabots*.

2. The combination of fibrous and elastic materials creates seats that are flexible and soft.

2

TRIAD

Use this simple set-by-step guide to make fun and environmentally friendly organizers
for cutlery, pens and pencils or paintbrushes.
Sections of bamboo and raffia in fresh, sharp colours make creating
these useful storage ideas child's play.

In the kitchen or the office,
Triad offers maximum effect from the most minimalist of design concepts.

DESIGN BY:
MARION DAVIAUD

TRIAD

TOOLBOX	
Tools	**Materials**
▪ Spring clamps ▪ Glue gun + glue sticks ▪ Sanding block + fine sandpaper ▪ Super glue ▪ Elbow paintbrush with handle	▪ 3 sections of bamboo cane of different heights and diameters ▪ Brightly coloured raffia (50g ball) ▪ Paint in a colour of your choice

Telling details: Coloured raffia adds a splash of colour to a practical idea that is simple, cheap and easy to make.

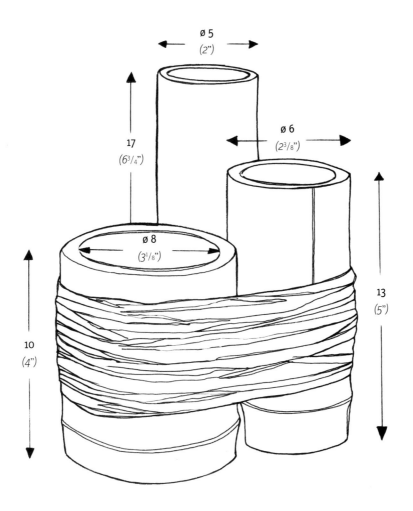

ø 5
(2")

ø 6
(2³/₈")

17
(6³/₄")

ø 8
(3¹/₈")

13
(5")

10
(4")

All measurements are in centimetres and inches (to nearest fraction).

Step-by-step-guide

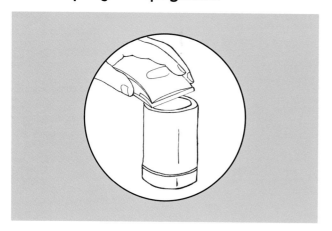

1. If necessary, sand the bamboo sections very lightly with fine sandpaper to soften the edges.

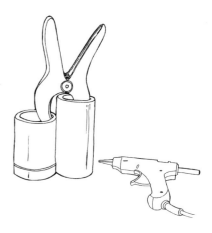

2. Assemble the bamboo sections using a glue gun. Use a spring clamp to hold them in position while they dry.

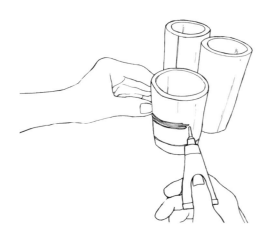

3. Put a spot of super glue on the end of the raffia.

4. Wind several thicknesses of raffia around the 3 pots, adding a few spots of super glue as you go.

5. Apply 2 coats of paint to the inside of the pots, using an elbow paintbrush to reach the bottom.

6. Whether in the kitchen or in a child's bedroom, *Triad* makes a versatile table or desk organizer with a multitude of potential uses.

EN POINTE

The *En Pointe* Table returns to the rural roots of traditional French craftsmanship, paying tribute to the traditional skills of the *feuillardiers* of rural south-west France, coopers who produced chestnut strips for wine barrels.

Put this little table beside the bed or the sofa to add a note of authentic rural character to your interiors.

DESIGN BY:
M&M DESIGNERS

STYLING BY:
ANNABEL GUERET *(EDMOND)*

EN POINTE

TOOLBOX	
Tools	**Materials**
▪ Radial arm saw ▪ Retractable knife ▪ Orbital sander ▪ Sewing needle + black thread ▪ Matches/lighter	▪ 6 x 2m *(6'7")* silver birch stakes (5-8cm *(2-3")* diameter) ▪ 2 black ratchet straps

Telling details: Quick and easy to make, this quirky little table offers all the beauty of silver birch bark with the rustic simplicity of tapered stakes.

ø 35 *(1' 1³/₄")* − 40 *(1' 3³/₄")*

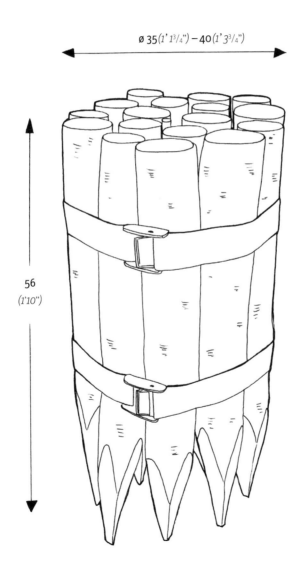

56
(1'10")

All measurements are in centimetres and inches (to nearest fraction).

Step-by-step-guide

1. Using a radial arm saw, cut the silver birch into 17 sections, each 56cm (1'10") long.

2. Taper one end of each stake: saw the first side, turn the stake through a quarter-turn to saw the second side, and repeat for the third and fourth sides.

3. Bunch the stakes together, place the ratchet straps around them and tighten them firmly.

4. Cut off the surplus ends of the straps with a retractable knife.

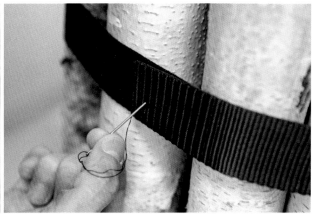

5. Burn the ends of the straps with a lighter to stop them fraying.

6. Put a stitch in the ends of the straps to secure them in lace.

7. Turn the table upside down and insert a few off-cuts from step 2 between the stakes to wedge them firmly.

8. Finish off by sanding the top.

M&M Designers
Martin Lévêque & Mathieu Maingourd

Martin & Mathieu in 7 dates

1999: They meet as students at the ESAA in Troyes.

2002: Mathieu works for Christian Dior and Céline.

2006: Martin moves to Brussels and works with designer Xavier Lust.

2008: Matheiu designs Do Pirate (alternative DIY project).

2010: Martin works with the architect Santiago Cirugeda's Recetas Urbanas practice in Seville pour l'agence. Mathieu goes freelance.

2012: Mathieu designs on-site games for a school in Senegal.

2013: They set up the Libre Objet collective (open-source design).

The distance between Nantes and Brussels is no object to M&M Designers, who regularly meet up to work on joint projects. Martin and Mathieu both have an inclusive, multi-disciplinary approach, both like to work at the outer limits of the design field, and both share the same philosophy: 'art and design, technical ingenuity and humanity' lie at the heart of their creations. Their approach to the environment and society naturally engenders an aesthetic of simplicity.

'Natural materials are highly expressive, and you just have to reveal them. Using raw materials, shapes and combinations, we are always trying to tell a story through our pieces, from their conception to the names we give them.

'For this book we have focused on natural treatments, such as the coir twine used in the Aloha coat stand, or scorched wood as an alternative to a classic paint finish in *Burnt Offering*. Only the *En Pointe* Table plays on the juxtaposition of the natural and the synthetic, in the form of the black ratchet straps.

'One of the things we wanted to do was to work with wood in the way traditional *feuillardiers* worked with chestnut in Martin's native region, rough-hewn and authentic, as can be seen in our series of designs using stakes. You have to accept the materials for what they are and work with them. Our aim was to make use of their shapes, structure and appearance to create fully functioning designs.

'From land art to the *feuillardiers*, from the Campana brothers to surfing culture, from Mario Merz to music, our sources of inspiration are varied and wide-ranging, and feed our creativity. Look, listen, observe: from the form of a snowflake to that of a grain of sand, our environment shapes our daily lives.'

Martin Lévêque
44, rue Eeckelaers – 1210 Bruxelles, Belgium
Tél.: +32 (0)4 85 78 55 19
martinlvqe@gmail.com – be.net/martinleveque

Mathieu Maingourd
math_ology@hotmail.com
be.net/math_ology
dopirate.free.fr

 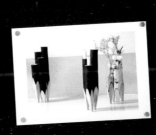  

From left to right: *Aloha* (p. 91) • *Burnt Offering* (p. 113) • *En Pointe* (p. 151) • *Sunrise* (p. 67)

SOBREIRO

DESIGN

Sobreiro is the Portuguese name for the cork oak tree.

For many years cork was used primarily for its impressive practical qualities,
mostly as an insulation material and in the wine industry.
Now its aesthetic qualities are increasingly being recognized,
and it is being used as a decorative element in furniture and other objects,
as designers vie with each other in using it to create natural and durable items to embellish interiors.

With its warm texture and colour and its softly filtered light,
Sobreiro offers lightness in every sense of the word.

DESIGN BY:
MARION DAVIAUD

TECHNICAL CONSULTANTS:
FALBALA LUMINAIRES

SOBREIRO

TOOLBOX

Tools

- Jigsaw + hacksaw
- Cordless drill
- Sanding block + fine sandpaper
- Electrical screwdriver + wire strippers
- Spring clamps
- Pair of compasses
- Metal rule
- Allen key
- Sewing needle
- Mini paint roller and small flat paintbrush

Materials

- 1 2m (6'7") roll cork sheet 52cm (1'8¹/₄") wide and 2mm (⁵/₆₄") thick
- 4m (13') red fabric cable + electrical components (cable clips, lamp holders, connector strips)
- 3 9W mini E14 energy-saving bulbs
- 3 x 15cm (6")-diameter lampshade ring sets
- Red paint
- 1m (3'3") aluminium tube (8mm (⁵/₁₆") diameter)
- 3 brass back plates (2.5cm (1") diameter)
- 1 sheet MDF (80 (2'8") x 60 (2') x 1cm (³/₈"))
- Clear or white nylon thread
- Cork adhesive + super glue

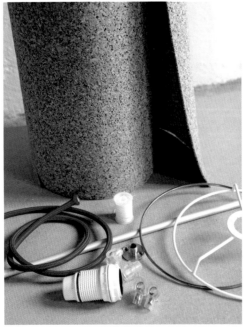

Telling details: Cork is not only 100 percent natural and recyclable, but it is also highly decorative, especially with the light filtering softly through its delicate pore structure.

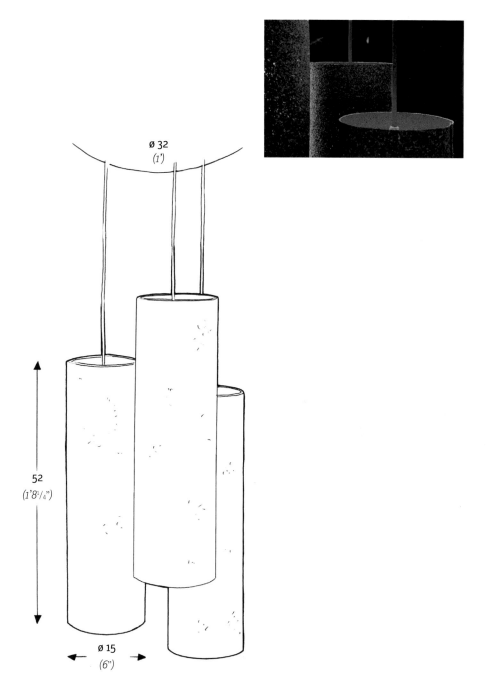

ø 32
(1')

52
(1'8¹/₄")

ø 15
(6")

All measurements are in centimetres and inches (to nearest fraction).

Step-by-step-guide

1. Cut 3 pieces of cork measuring 50cm *(1'7¼")* x 49.5cm *(1'6½")* (circumference of the lampshade ring + 2cm *(¾")* margin).

2. Paint one side, applying the paint lightly so that it does not seep through the pores.

3. Divide the fabric cable into 3 lengths to attach the lampholders. Strip back the fabric and glue it, the strip the electrical wires back by 5mm *(³⁄₁₆")* using wire strippers (as in steps 7 to 9 of Sunrise, pp. 71–2).

4. Attach the stripped cable end to the lamp holder connections. Insert the wires in the connections and screw in firmly with a screwdriver. Draw the cable back so the connection rests in the fitting and screw the two parts of the fitting together.

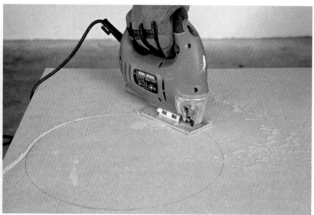

5. Saw a 32cm *(1')*-diameter circle of MDF and sand it. This will serve as a ceiling rose to conceal the cables, with metallic tubing serving as spacers.

6. On the circle, mark where the positions of the cables and screws for attaching to the ceiling (black crosses and red asterisks respectively in the photo).

7. Drill holes of the right diameter for your cable and screws. Countersink them on the other side to accommodate the screw heads.

8. Draw a line 2cm *(³/₄")* from the vertical edge of each piece of cork sheet, and overlap with the other end. Hold in place with spring clamps.

Step-by-step-guide

9. Glue along the length of the tube with a strong cork adhesive.

10. To strengthen the join, sew a few stitches down the length of it, tie them off and add a drop of clear glue to the knots.

11. For the spacers, saw 3 x 3cm (1¹/₈") lengths of aluminium tubing. Check that your screws are long enough to screw securely into the ceiling fixings.

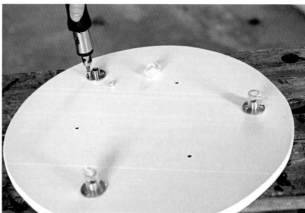

12. Fix the back plates at the points where the cable will pass through and screw the cable clips on top of them.

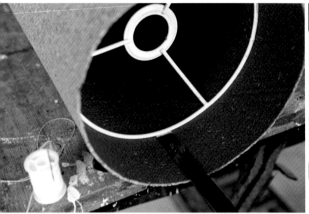

13. Position the lampshade rings 5cm *(2")* in from the ends, then attach them to the glue with 4 simple knots. Repeat on all the lampshade rings. Insert the bulbs. Although cork in its natural state is a fire-retardant, take care to use low energy bulbs.

14. Pass the 3 red cables through the MDF ceiling rose, check the heights, then tighten the cable clips with an Allen key.

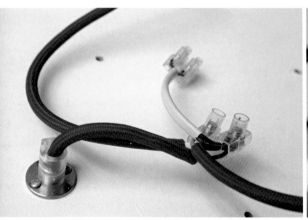

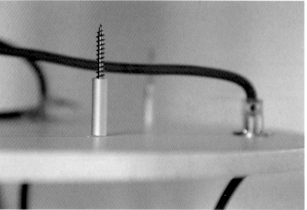

15. Connect the wires to the connector. Connect another cable with a connector at the other end to connect the whole light to the electrical supply in the ceiling. The connector must be large enough to receive several wires.

16. Attach the MDF ceiling rose to the ceiling with screws between the spacers.

SWING

Take inspiration from a child's swing to make these imaginative hanging shelves.

Use reclaimed wood or rough-sawn oak and hemp rope to retain all the authentic character of the wood and stay 100 percent natural.

DESIGN BY:
AURÉLIE DROUET

SWING

TOOLBOX

Tools

- Ruler
- Circular saw
- Cordless drill
- Clamps
- Orbital sander
- Spirit level

Materials

- 3 x 120cm *(3'11")* boards rough-sawn oak (45 *(1'5³/₄")* x 3cm *(1¹/₈")*)
- 16m *(52')* x 1.2cm *(¹/₂")* diameter hemp rope (adjust according to your requirements)
- 4 zinc-plated steel screw eyes (2.5cm *(1")* diameter) + rawlplugs

Telling details: A light, airy design in silvery wood and pale hemp — pretty and 100 percent natural.

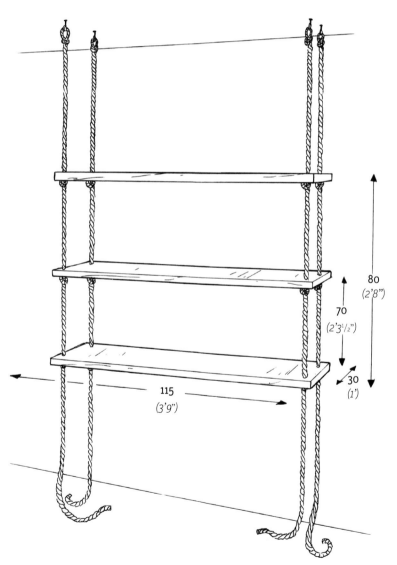

80
(2'8")

70
(2'3½")

30
(1')

115
(3'9")

All measurements are in centimetres and inches (to nearest fraction).

Step-by-step-guide

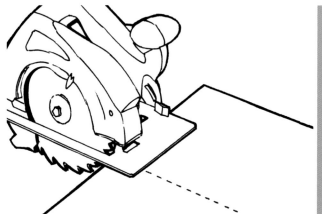

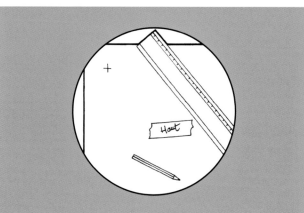

1. Measure the boards and saw them to the dimensions on the plans, taking care to keep one rough edge per plank.

2. On one of the boards mark the positions of the ropes, around 3.5cm *(1¼")* from the ends.

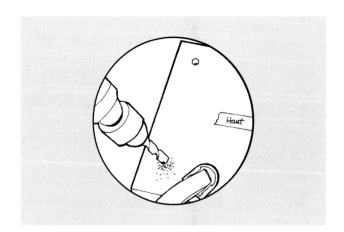

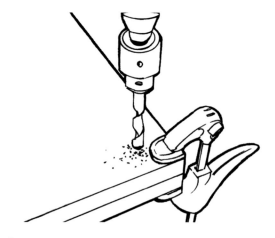

3. Drill the holes with a wood bit with a larger diameter than the rope (here 1.5cm *(⅝")*). This board will serve as a guide for drilling the holes in the other boards.

4. Position the second board precisely under the first and secure it with clamps. Drill, then repeat with the last board.

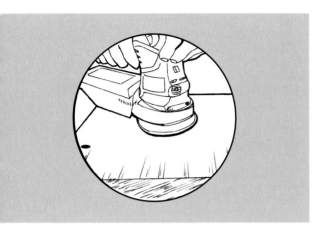

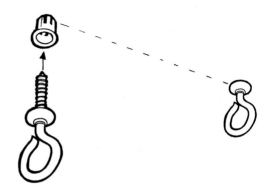

5. Sand the boards very lightly to retain their rugged appearance.

6. Mark the positions of the screw eyes on the ceilings and attach them with rawlplugs appropriate to your ceiling. Take care to ensure that the screw eyes are positioned so that the inner edges of the boards rest against the wall.

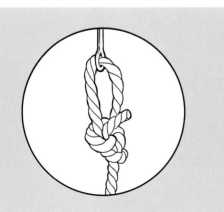

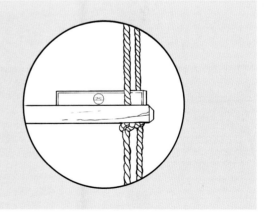

7. Divide the rope into 4 equal lengths and tie them securely to the screw eyes with a knot such as a bowline. Tape the ends of the rope to stop them fraying and to make it easier to pass them through the holes.

8. Pass the 4 ropes through the first shelf and adjust the height. Use a spirit level to check it is horizontal before knotting the rope under each of the holes. Repeat for the other shelves (two people are needed to adjust the shelves).

Cork
Antoine Phelouzat, designer

The Cork collection has its origins at the point where tradition meets design. From the *Buto* stool to the *Cork&Craft* baskets, these pieces charm us with their solidity and their lightness. Antoine Phelouzat uses cork to surprise and to question: 'Contact with the material and with the people who work it was essential for me: it's not just the tradition that interests me, but also the ways in which skills adapt and change.'

INSPIRED BY MILKING STOOLS AND WOBBLY TOYS, THE BUTO STOOL PLAYS WITH NOTIONS OF BALANCE, ITS SINGLE LEG WEIGHTED WITH STEEL TO ENSURE IT STAYS UPRIGHT.

THE GENEROUS CURVES OF THE PIECES IN THE CORK&CRAFT SERIES BEAR WITNESS TO THE BEST TRADITIONS OF CRAFTSMANSHIP IN CORK.

After working with the Brinkworth Design Ltd and Tom Dixon in London and the Noé Duchaufour-Lawrence agency, Antoine Phelouzat founded his own design studio in 2005. His creations reflect his approach to design: 'An object should be a vector of value, of knowledge. It should prompt questions, awaken curiosity. A product is interesting when it offers different layers of understanding.'

Antoine Phelouzat
208, rue Saint-Maur – 75010 Paris, France
Tel: +33 (0)6 87 80 02 49
antoine@ant-1.com – antoinephelouzat.com

1. Made by Agglolux-CBL in the Landes region of France, these pieces are produced by Gallery S. Bensimon.

2. The materials: cork and steel.

1

2

APPENDICES

Crochet tutorial – the basic stitches

Pattern for the Crochet pouffe

Aloha: building the basic structure

Address book

Glossary

Opposite: *Cluster of vases by M&M Designers (see pp.112–17)*

CROCHET TUTORIAL – THE BASIC STITCHES

▪ Chain stitch (ch)

Bring the yarn over the crochet hook from front to back (yarn over) (1), then draw it back through the loop (2) to make a chain stitch (3).

1.   2.   3.

▪ Slip stitch (sl st)

Insert the crochet hook in the loop as shown (1), yarn over (2). Bring the yarn back through the loop (3), then through the loop on the hook (4).

1.   2.   3.   4.

▪ Double crochet (dc)

Insert the crochet hook in the loop as shown (1), yarn over (2). Draw the yarn back through the loop (3), yarn over (4). Draw the yarn through the 2 loops on the hook (5) to finish (6).

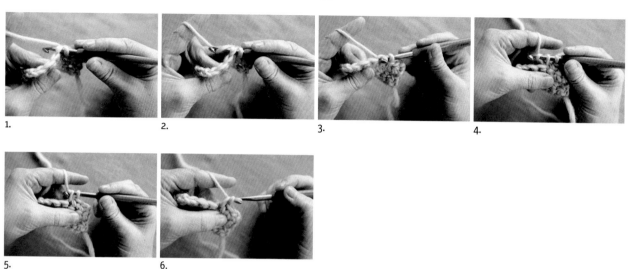

1.

2.

3.

4.

5.

6.

▪ Treble crochet (tr)

Yarn over (1), insert the crochet hook in the loop as shown (2). Yarn over (3), draw the yarn through the loop (4). Yarn over (5), draw the yarn back through 2 loops (6). Yarn over (7), draw the yarn through the 2 remaining loops (8).

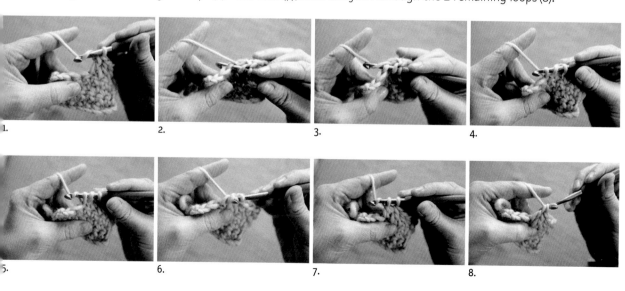

1.

2.

3.

4.

5.

6.

7.

8.

POP'OUF Pouffe (see p. 41)

Pattern

 Centre ring

• Slip stitch (sl st)

 Chain stitch (ch)

 Double crochet (dc)

 2 double crochets in one double crochet

 Popcorn stitch at start of row (with first treble crochet = 3 chain stitches)

 Popcorn stitch with 5 treble crochets

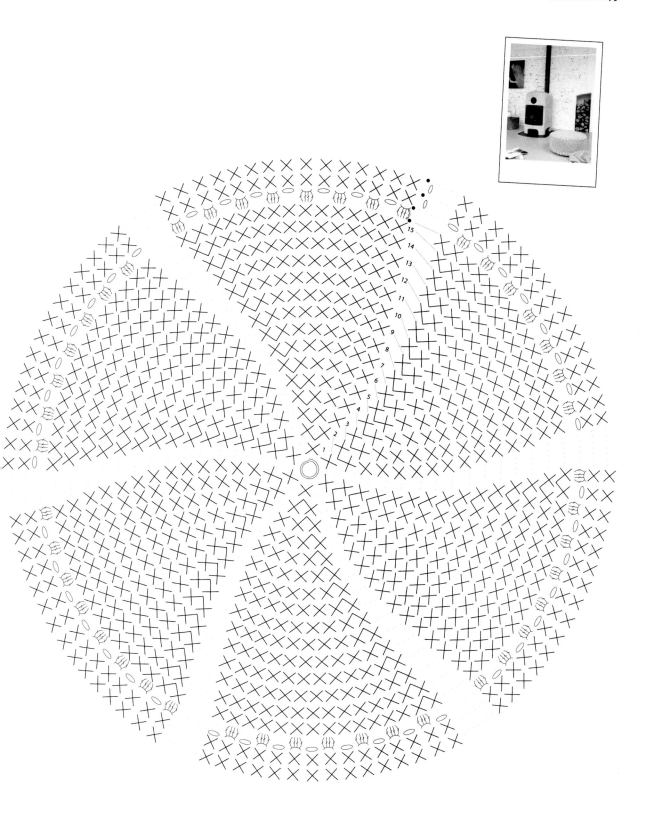

1
2
3
4
5
6
7
8
9
10
11
12
13
14
15

ALOHA (see p. 91)

Building the basic structure.

Build the basic structure on the floor (cf. step 4, p. 94). To determine the angles of the first 3 bamboo canes, follow the dimensions on the diagram: place n°1 on n°2, then n°3 on the first 2, and tape them all together.

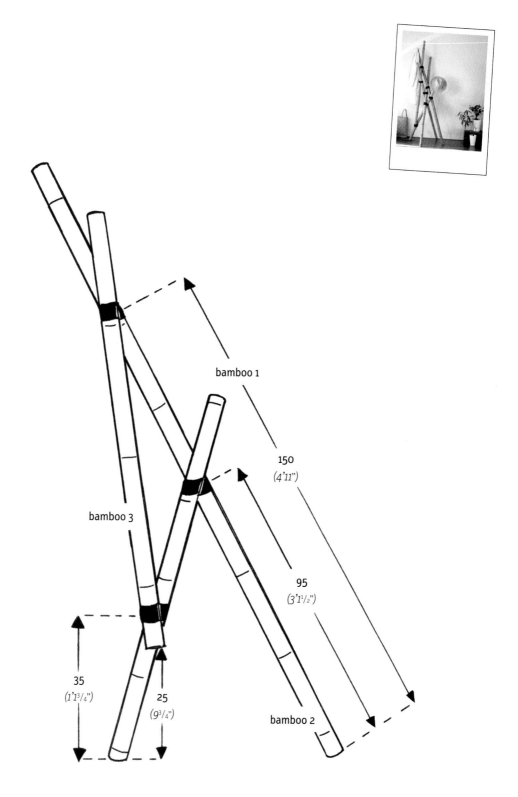

bamboo 1

150
(4'11")

95
(3'1¹/₂")

bamboo 3

35
(1'1³/₄")

25
(9³/₄")

bamboo 2

All measurements are in centimetres and inches (to nearest fraction).

CONTRIBUTOR'S ADDRESS BOOK

■ **Atelier du petit parc**
(photos p. 34 & 130)
19, allée baco – 44000 Nantes
Tel: +33 (0)6 89 29 17 17
contact@atelierdupetitparc.fr
atelierdupetitparc.fr

■ **Atelier La Cabane**
(photos p. 8)
42, rue Jean Yole – 85350 Île d'Yeu
contact@mariedelile.com
mariedelile.com

■ **Bloomingville**
(vases, photos p. 6 & 150)
bloomingville.com

■ **Edmond, Annabel Gueret**
Interior designer
(photos p. 40, 112 ¶ 150)
annabel@edmond.tm.fr

■ **Jérémy Boche**
Landscape designer
(construction of *Lumberjack* Chairs, p. 59)
Nantes
Tel: +33 (0)6 12 13 20 16

■ **Maill0**
(lace baskets, photo p. 6)
17, rue du grand Logis – 44190 Clisson
Tel: +33 (0)2 28 21 39 15
veronique.damart@free.fr
mmaillo.blogspot.fr
maillo-design.com

DESIGNS

Swing Shelves

■ **Frédéric Mazère**
(small photos)
mazerefrederic@gmail.com
fredmazere.blogspot.fr

■ **Janik Coat**
(portrait of woman)
janikcoat@gmail.com
janikkinaj.free.fr

■ **MUJI**
(recycled paper animals)
www.muji.eu

Bambouseraie Pouffe

■ **Nathalie Lété**
(Forêt noire wallpaper from Domestic)
nathalie@nathalie-lete.com
nathalie-lete.com
Tel: +33 (0)1 49 60 84 76

Loom Child's Chair

■ **Atelier du petit parc**
(screen, suitcases & vintage stoneware bottle)

■ **Audrey Jeanne**
(postcard)
ilovedrawing@orange.fr – audreyjeanne.fr

■ **Happy to see you**
(rag doll)
109, route du Château d'Olonne
85100 Les Sables d'Olonne
Tel: +33 (0)2 51 32 67 50
happytoseeyou.fr

■ **Molly Flowers**
(paper pompoms and floral tote)
contact@mollyflowers.fr
atelierdupetitparc.fr

Pajaro clothes Rail

■ **Atelier du petit parc**
(vintage wicker chair)

■ **Monsieur et Madame sont au salon**
(porcelain swallows)
Tel: +33 (0)6 27 54 70 30
jcdlebagousse@sfr.fr
madameausalon.canalblog.com

■ **Sophie Morille**
(cushion)
sophiemorille@gmail.com
sophiemorille.blogspot.fr

Burnt Offering Candlestick

■ **La Cerise**
(deer)
16, passage d'Orléans – 44000 Nantes
Tel: +33 (0)2 40 74 57 33
fbinvel@lacerise-nantes.com
lacerise-nantes.com

■ **Delphine Vaute**
(framed illustration)
delphvaute@hotmail.com
delphinegribouille.ultra-book.com
delphinevaute.hautetfort.com

Pop'Ouf Pouffe

■ **Wanted Paris**
(photograph on wall by Wendy Bevan)
23, rue du roi de Sicile – 75004 Paris
Tel: +33 (0)1 44 54 02 55
contact@wantedparis.com
wantedparis.com

■ **Weltevree**
(wood burner)
www.weltevreeshop.nl

En Pointe Table

■ **Bloomingville**
(green vase)
bloomingville.com

■ **Caravane**
(eiderdown)
6, rue Pavée – 75004 Paris
Tel: +33 (0)1 44 61 04 20
caravane@caravane.fr
caravane.fr

■ **Serendipity**
(round Mercer cushions)
81-83, rue du Cherche-midi – 75006 Paris
Tel: +33 (0)1 40 46 01 15
contact@serendipity.fr
serendipity.fr

Triad desk organisers

■ **Gabijo**
(biodegradable cutlery)
19, rue de la Tannerie
97421 La Rivière Saint Louis
Tel: +33 (0)2 62 45 42 03
www.gabijo.fr

Vasco Standard Lamp

■ **Edmond, Annabel Gueret**
Créateur d'intérieurs
(three-legged stool)

Zéphyr Door Curtain

■ **Atelier du petit parc**
(demijohns)

Bench

■ **Les Enfants du Brok**
(Makiko Hicher ceramic cups)
18 rue Gutenberg – 44100 Nantes

Tel: +33 (0)2 49 44 78 32
contact@lesenfantsdubrok.com
lesenfantsdubrok.com

DESIGNER PROFILES

Sand

■ **Victor Castanera**
castanerav@gmail.com
victorcastanera.com
Tel: + 34 664 350 553

Rattan

■ **Métalobil**
ZA Champ Fleuri
15 rue des coquelicots
44840 Les Sorinières
Tel: +33 (0)2 40 69 56 03
clic@metalobil.fr
metalobil.fr

■ **TETRARC**
19 bis, rue La Noue Bras de Fer
44200 NANTES
Tel: +33 (0)2 40 89 46 26
agence@tetrarc.fr
tetrarc.fr

Straw

■ **Tété Knecht**
ttknecht@bluewin.ch
teteknecht.com

<u>Cork</u>

- **Antoine Phelouzat**
208, rue Saint-Maur – 75010 Paris
Tel: 06 87 80 02 49
antoine@ant-1.com
antoinephelouzat.com

- **Hugues Lawson-Body – Photographe**
hugueslawsonoffice@gmail.com
hugueslawsonbody.com

WEBSITES OF INTEREST

- **A Bird's Leap**
www.abirdsleap.com/2013/02/diy-bamboo-ladder.html

- **Casa.com.br**
http://casa.abril.com.br/materia/pufe-ecologico-pneu-descartado-corda-sisal#9

- **Crafts with jars**
www.craftswithjars.com/2013/06/15-mason-jar-herb-gardens.html

- **Ernest est céleste**
http://ernestestceleste.canalblog.com/archives/2012/09/28/25201240.html

- **Esprit Cabane**
www.espritcabane.com/decoration/idees-deco/abat-jour-bambou/

- **Flax & Twine**
www.flaxandtwine.com/2012/02/woven-finger-knitting-hula-hoop-rug-diy.html

- **Madame Ki**
www.madameki.fr/archives/2012/04/17/23986316.html

- **Made by Girl**
http://madebygirl.blogspot.fr/2010/08/my-diy-moooi-pendant-light-in-progress.html

- **Organisation Mariage**
www.organisation-mariage.net/boule-de-rotin.htm

- **Patrick Nadeau**
www.patricknadeau.com

- **Sheterness**
www.shelterness.com/cozy-diy-crocheted-lampshade/

- **Sophie Pinard**
www.sophiepinard.com

- **Sweet French Toast**
www.sweetfrenchtoast.com/2012/03/05/how-to-diy-barn-door-headboard/

GLOSSARY

Blind hole
Hole that doesn't pass through the full depth of the material.

Cable clamp
Part creating a secure joint between cable and lampholder. For safety reasons, it is important to avoid exerting direct pressure on even the simplest of electrical connections: the cable clamp transfers the weight to the outer sheath of the cable.

Chamfer
To cut a surface at an angle.

Clamp
Tool for holding part in position temporarily during assembly or construction.

Countersink
A conical hole cut into a surface or the cutter used to make the hole, which allows the head of a screw to sit flush with or below the surface.

Electrical cable
Electrical wires grouped together and covered by an insulating sheath, available in sizes ranging from 0.75mm upwards.

Fabric cable
Covered electric cable, using many materials including rayon, polyester, cotton, linen, hemp and even paper or metal.

Glue
To cover a surface with glue.

Lost-head nail
Long slim nail with a small head, used principally in woodwork.

MDF
Medium Density Fibreboard.

Nut
A joining device with a threaded hole.

Nut and bolt
Nuts and bolts screw together to fasten two or more parts together.

Pilot hole (pre-drilled)
Pre-drilled hole making it easier to insert screws and nails.

Stripping back
Using wire strippers to strip back the insulating sheath from electrical wires.

Template
A one-to-one scale pattern used in construction.

Threaded rod
Rods, wholly or partly threaded, available in a wide range of metals, diameters and threads.

ACKNOWLEDGEMENTS

To all the designers who contributed to this book, for their advice and generosity.

To everyone else who made it possible, from the landscape designer to Jean-Luc.

To our suppliers and partners for their support: BDF-Globstor, Déco-Nature, Falbala Luminaires, Garnstudio Drops Design, Les Toisons Bretonnes, Naturellement Chanvre, Ripolin and the Ville de Nantes.

And to the natural beauties of Pénestin in Brittany.

PHOTO CREDITS

PHOTOGRAPHIES

© Jérôme Blin, except for the following pages,
- p. 8, © Mariedelîle
- p. 74-75, © Rosa Álvarez de Arcaya/Victor Castanera
- p. 110, © Métalobil
- p. 142-143, © Andrés Otero
- p. 172-173, © Hugues Lawson-Body

DESIGNS

p. 67, 91, 113, 151 & 175, Copyleft: This work may be freely copied, distributed or transformed according to the terms of the Free Art Licence (www.artlibre.org).

ILLUSTRATIONS

Jean-Marie Reymond

STYLING

Annabel Gueret, atelier du petit parc & Aurélie Drouet

PAINTS

Ripolin

Published by Scriptum Editions, 2016

An imprint of Co & Bear Productions (UK) Ltd

63 Edith Grove, London, SW10 0LB

www.scriptumeditions.co.uk

PUBLISHERS: Beatrice Vincenzini & Francesco Venturi

COVER DESIGN: Mr Cat

TRANSLATION: Barbara Mellor

EDITORIAL: Juliette de Lavaur, Françoise Mathay & Marion Dellapina

GRAPHIC DESIGN: Gaëlle Chartier, Sabine Houplain, Claire Mieyeville & Audrey Lorel

Distributed by Thames & Hudson

10 9 8 7 6 5 4 3 2 1

ISBN: 978–1–902686–84–4

First published, in French, by Editions du Chêne – Hachette Livre, 2014

Original title: *100% Déco: Design Nature, faites vos meubles*

©Editions du Chêne – Hachette Livre, 2014, for the original work.

Translation ©Co&Bear Productions (UK) Ltd